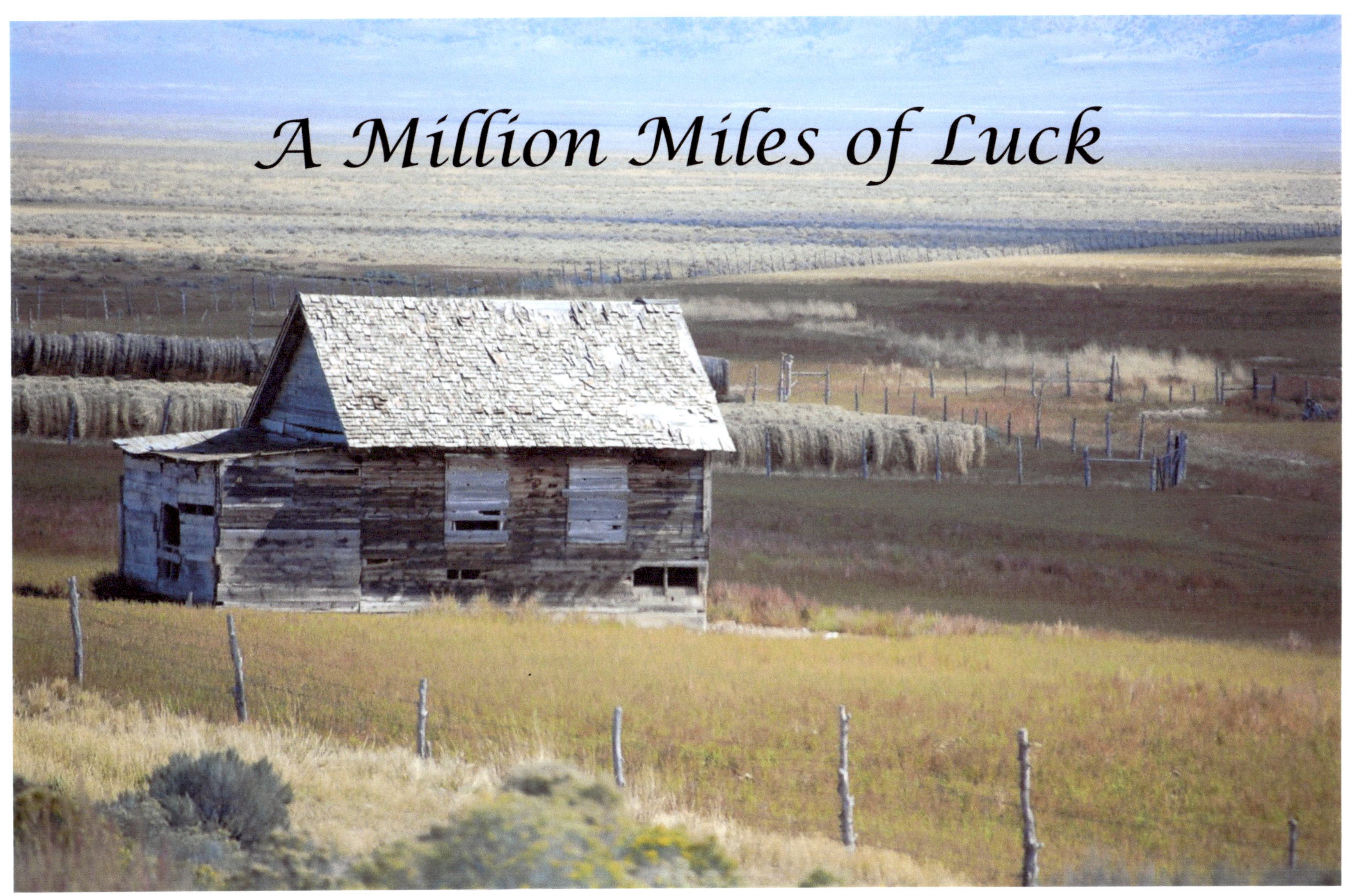

Copyright 2021 by Judy Foster

ISBN: 978-0-578-30218-8

Special thanks to my dad and mom for instilling in me my desire to travel and see our beautiful country.

Thank you to Lorraine Sobson for editing this book.

Jetlaunch and Chris O'Byrne for formatting the book.

Rich Selby for printing it.

Forward

A million miles of luck. Well, you know that cannot be literal. I haven't walked a million miles, nor do I have that on my backside sitting in any and all forms of travel.

That said, there are thousands of miles for sure. I have been blessed with having been to all 50 states three times—with the exception of Hawaii; I have only been there twice. My husband and I have been to all the National Parks you can drive to in the continental United States. I am not bragging I am merely stating facts.

The title of this book comes from a different place: a place of great gratitude for all of the things that I have been able to witness through the lens of my camera. The greatness of mountains, the vast oceans, from the largest of creatures to the smallest. Creatures that walk, fly, slither, and swim have been seen and admired.

A long time ago I was told that "the harder you work the luckier you get." For a long time, I thought that was the silliest thing I had ever heard. I mean, luck has nothing to do with the kind of preparation that builds skill … right? You practice, you learn, you try, you do, and that is what makes us successful.

Well, it wasn't until I took my photography more seriously that I started to understand. I used to see pictures in the *National Geographic* where the photographer stated that it took them days of sitting in a blind during all kinds of adversity to get a shot. I thought to myself, "I would never do such a crazy thing." And, honestly, I still haven't gone to such extremes.

I have however, thousands of miles with my camera strapped to me. I have taken hundreds if not thousands of pictures that didn't work out—but I keep walking and I keep shooting. I can take a shot and go back to the same location over and over at the same time of day hoping to get another shot. You are always looking to "best" the last shot. The funny thing is that animals—although creatures of habit—don't have the same timetable. Each day their routine can vary by minutes or hours. A flock of a certain type of bird will spend only so much time in an area and then they move on. If you weren't there you've missed them until next year. If you didn't get the shot, too bad. So, again it's all about perseverance and a lot of luck.

Perseverance is one of the greatest qualities we all need. It gets us through whatever life throws at us. The ability to keep on keeping on regardless of how we feel and what we think is the key to getting what we want. One foot in front of the other. Not giving up no matter what. It is through persevering and not giving up where the "luck" is found.

So, to you, my friends I can only say: Stay the course. Because the harder you work, the luckier you'll get.

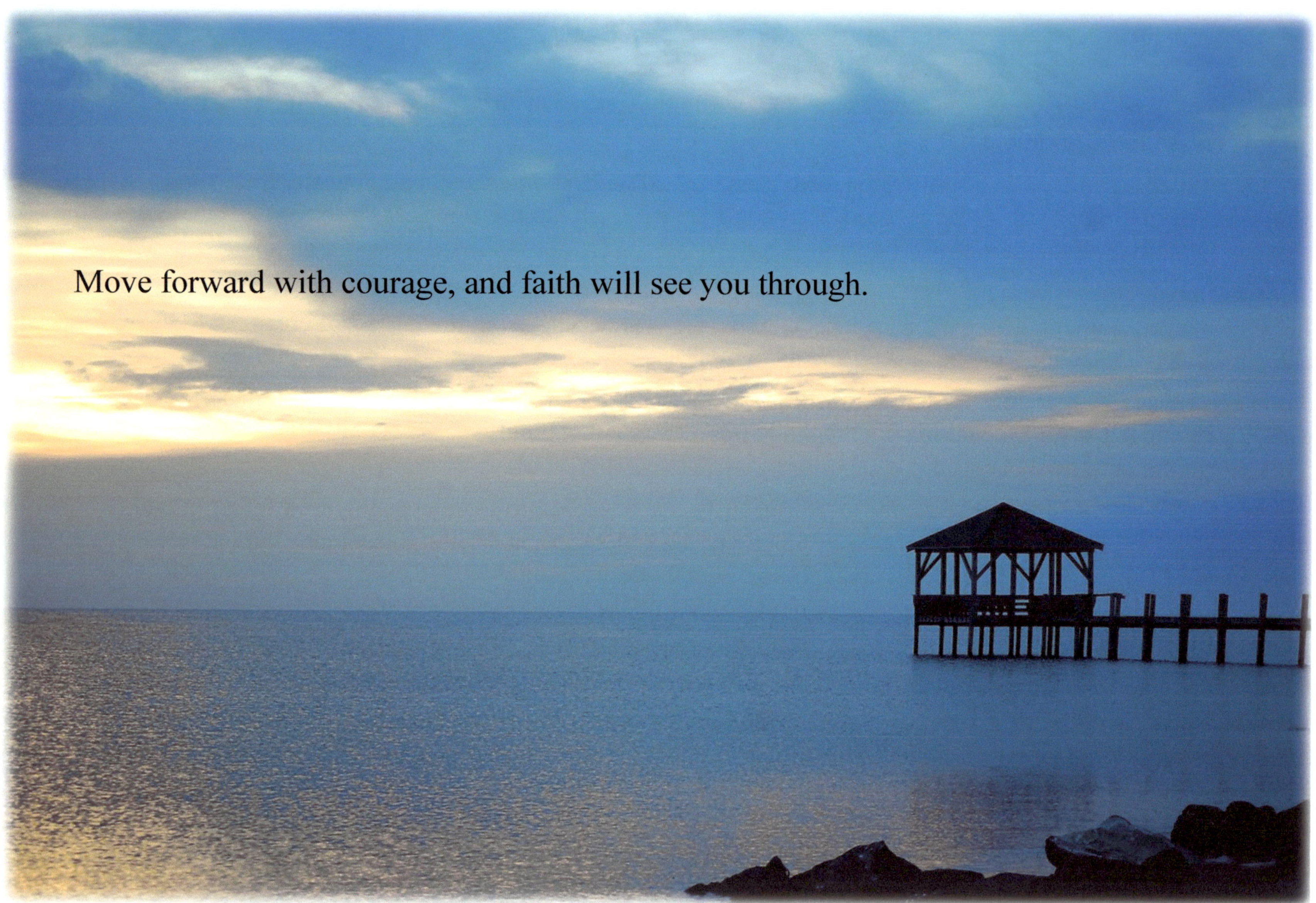
Move forward with courage, and faith will see you through.

Give yourself permission to:

Walk in the rain

Sing

Laugh

Tell a silly joke

Stroll down a country lane

Ask a "stupid" question

Take a nap

Watch a rerun for the tenth time

Eat cake

Love someone

Forgive someone

Forgive yourself

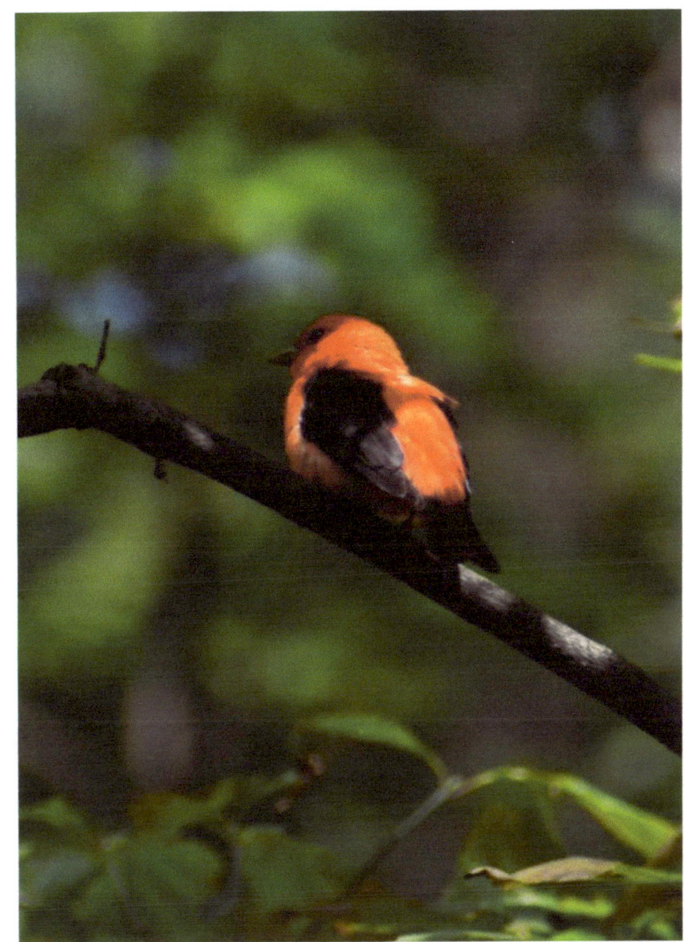

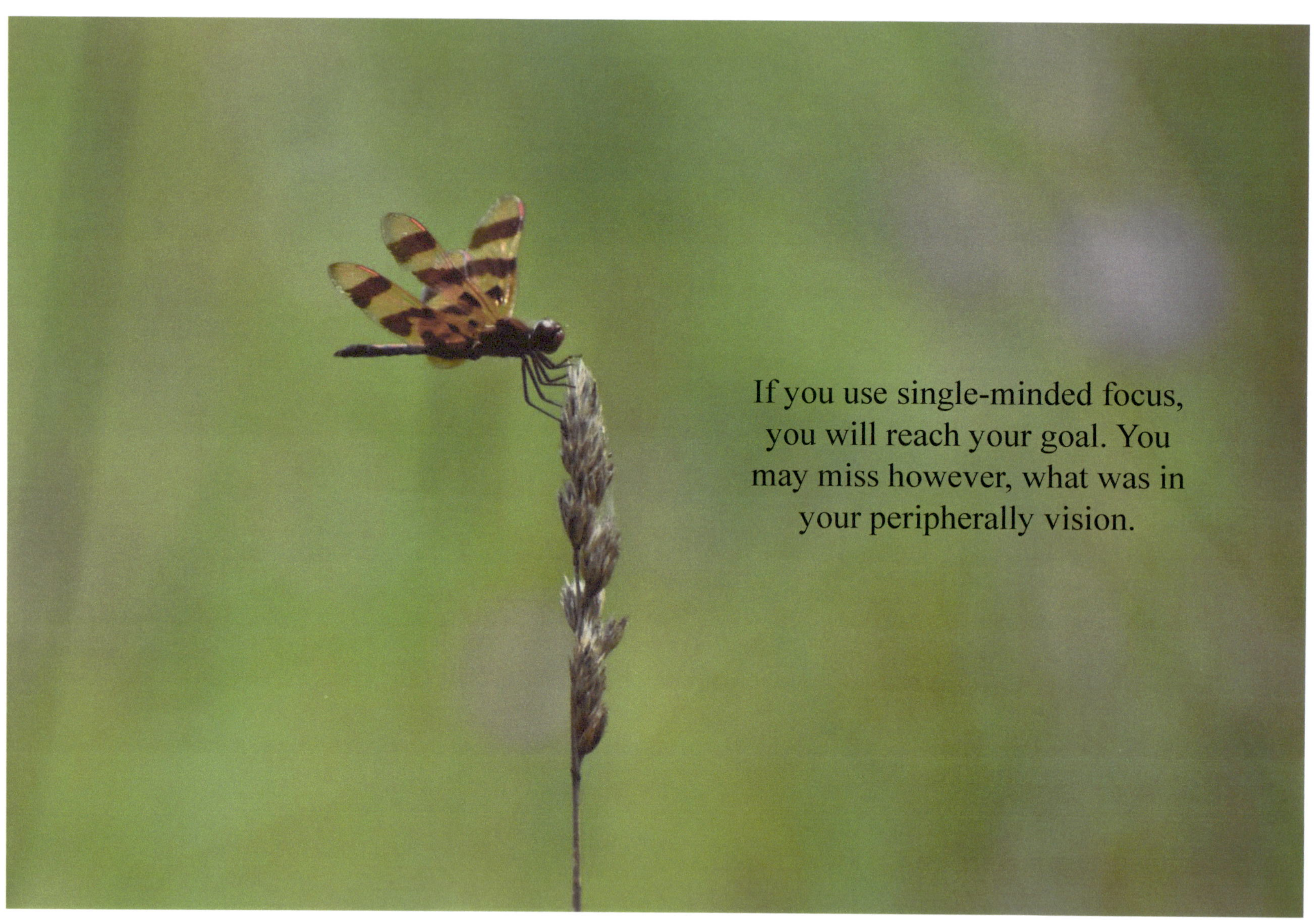

If you use single-minded focus,
you will reach your goal. You
may miss however, what was in
your peripherally vision.

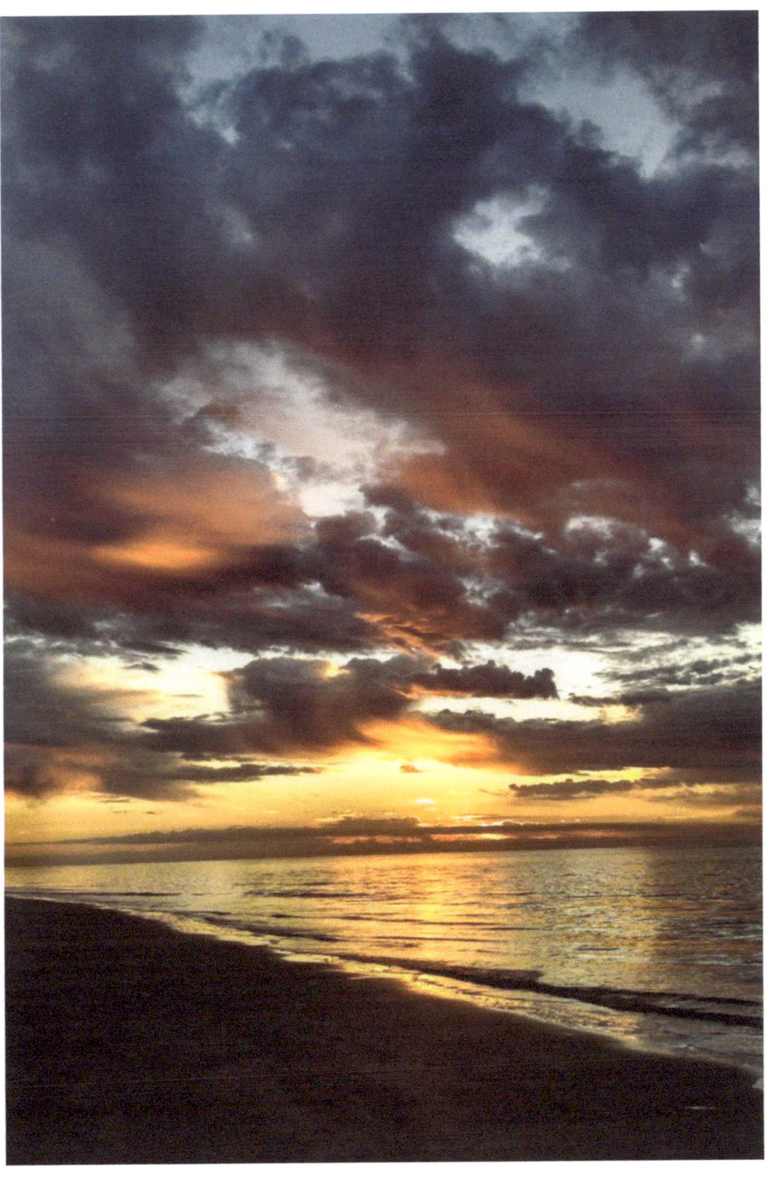

There is something about this ocean—only this one, the Atlantic—that stirs my emotions like nothing else. I feel small and insignificant and yet powerful and totally at peace. It fills me with great joy and wonder.

The saddest day for me is always the day that I leave the ocean. I make sure I get up for sunrise to say my goodbye. This year the sunrise was spectacular! —the prettiest I had ever seen.

As I finished filling my heart, I turned to see a man and his dog. The dog came right over to me. As I was loving it up, the man told me that this would be his dog's last sunrise.

It was then I realized this magnificent sunrise wasn't for me, but for him. God wanted him to see what a beautiful world he was about to enter. Nice going, God.

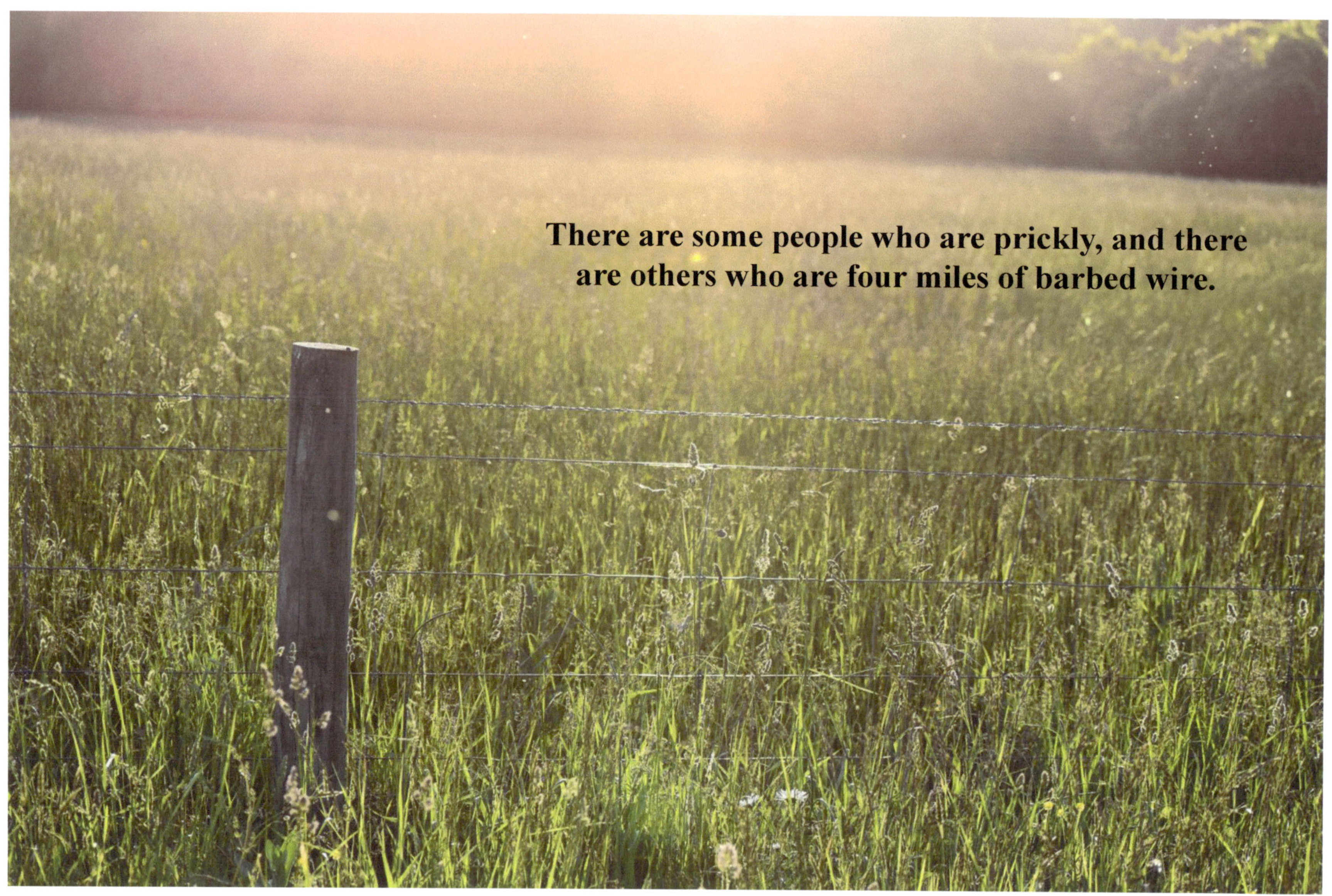
There are some people who are prickly, and there
are others who are four miles of barbed wire.

When a plant becomes rootbound it cannot grow. It is only when the roots are given a chance to expand and shift that the plant will thrive again. When a person spends all their time worrying about what is below in their "dirt," they become rootbound as well. Growth only happens when you learn from your mistakes, change your situation, and expand your horizons.

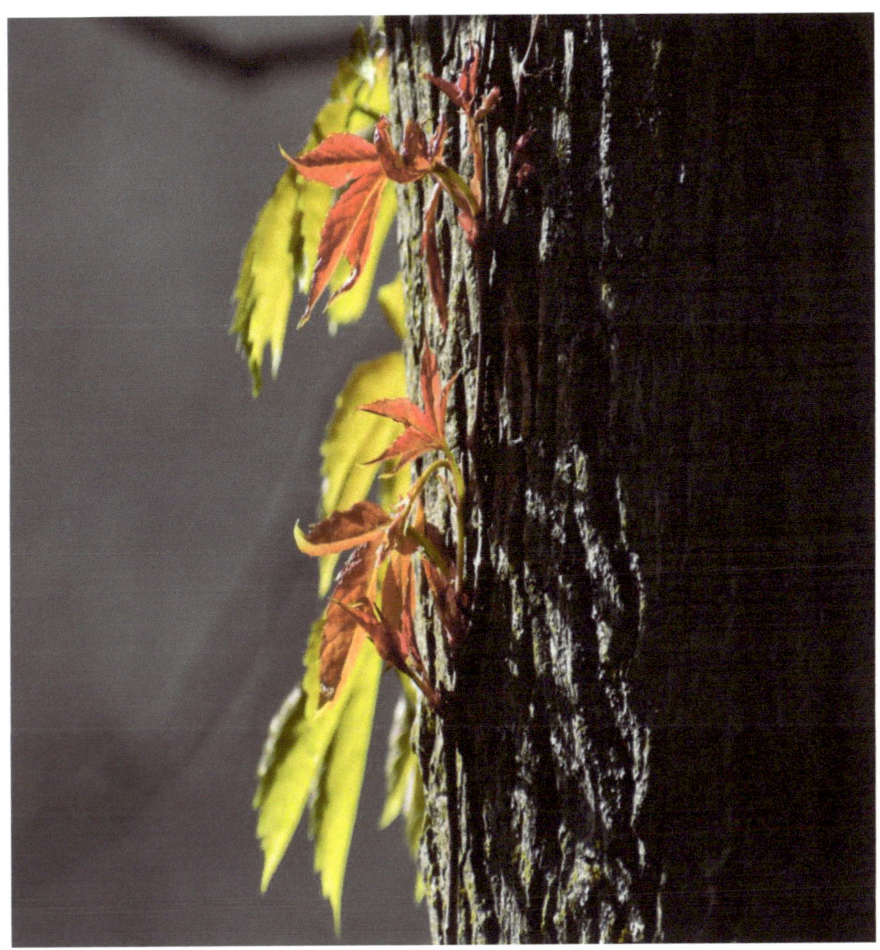

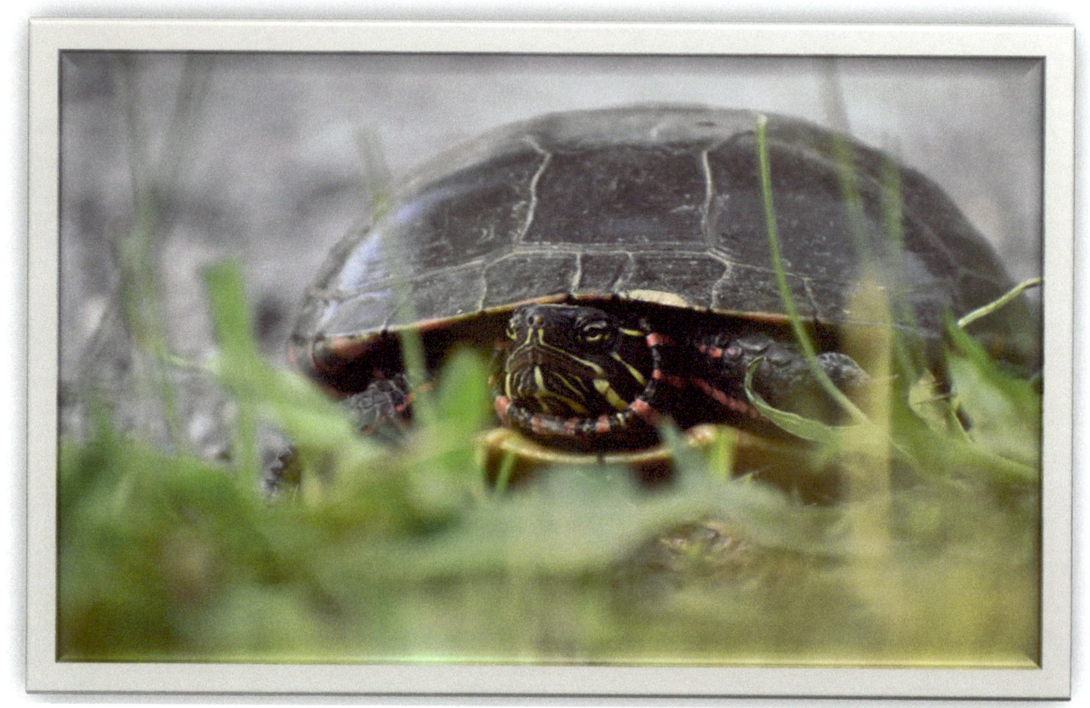

Just because you have the same size shoe as someone else doesn't mean you'll be comfortable in their shoes or vice versa. We all wear them a little differently.

Wisdom is not born from intelligence. It comes from examining the lesson that life gives you from every angle, learning and understanding the lesson and moving forward.

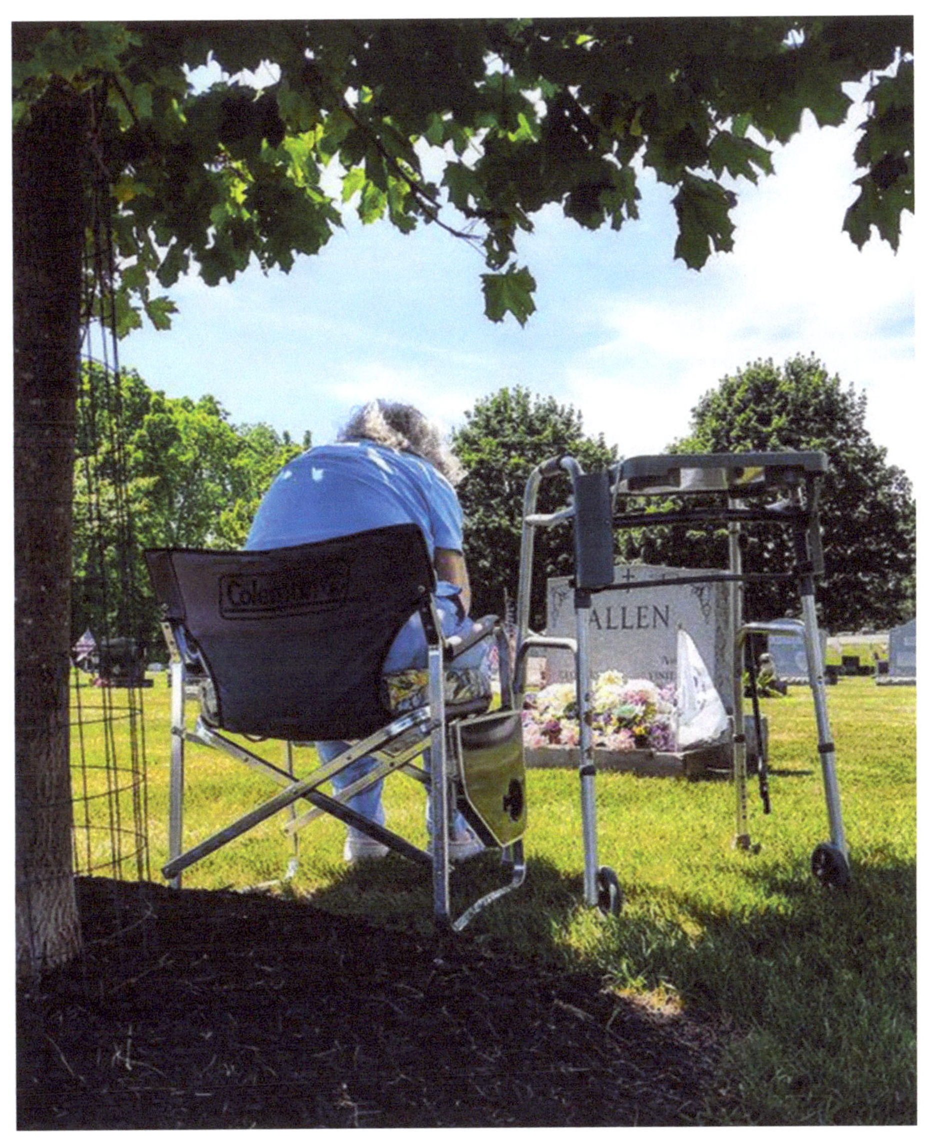

Love:

Fearlessly

Openly

Unconditionally

Happily

Forever

My wish for young girls:

May you have the fortitude of a cowgirl

The gentleness of a fawn

The strength of a lioness

The wisdom of Ruth Bader Ginsburg

And the fearlessness of a Disney Princess

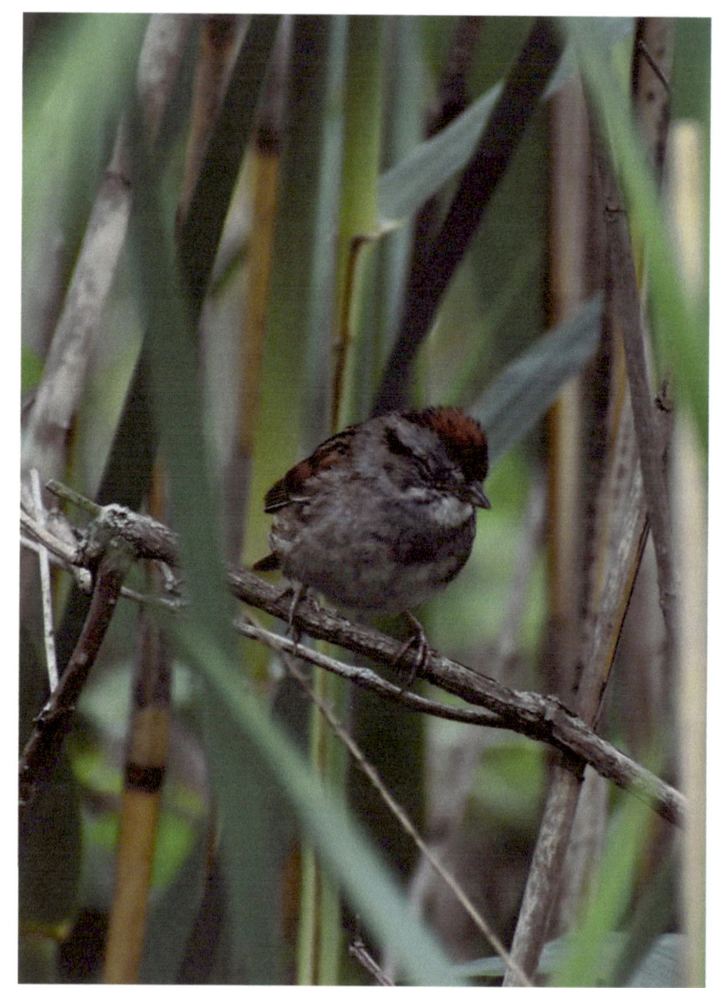

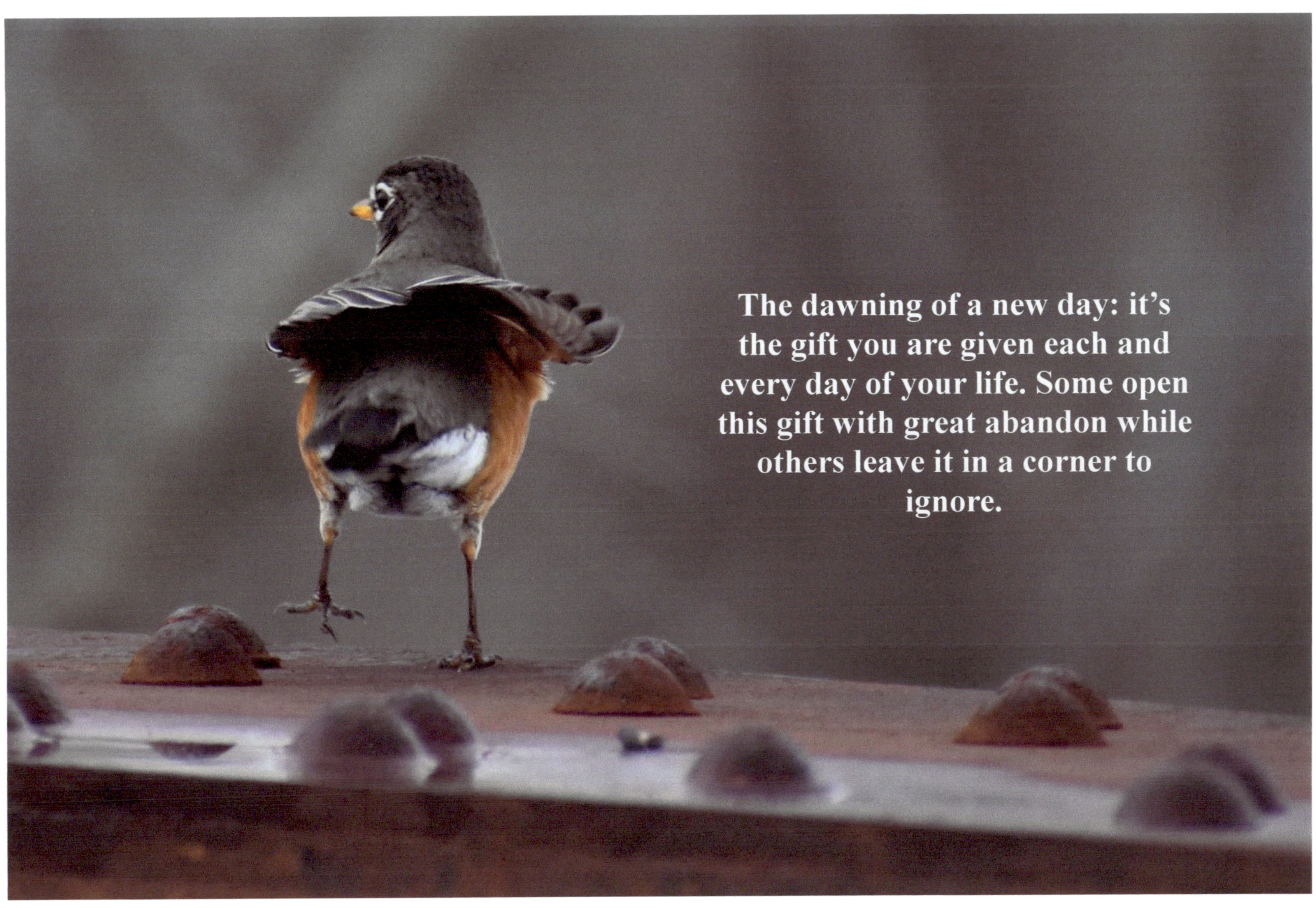

The dawning of a new day: it's the gift you are given each and every day of your life. Some open this gift with great abandon while others leave it in a corner to ignore.

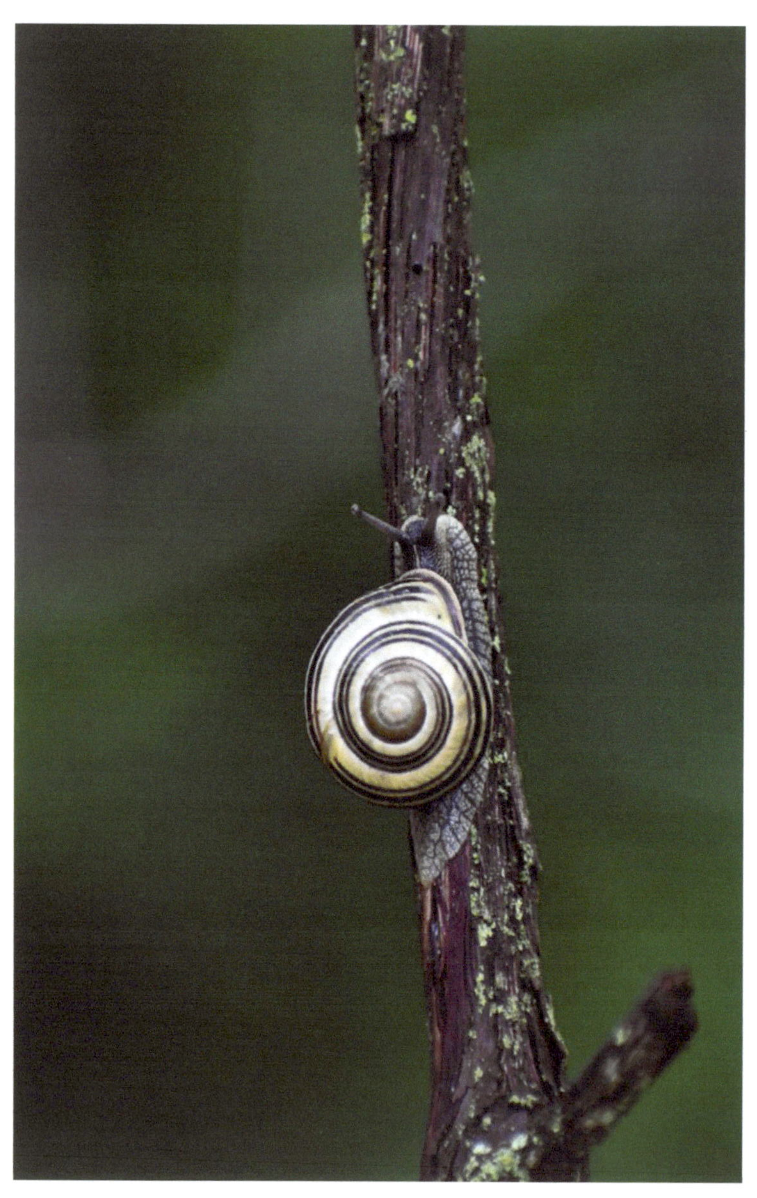

My wish for young boys:

May you have the confidence of an eagle

The humbleness of an ant

The courage of a lion

The gentleness of a lamb

And the mindfulness of Buddha

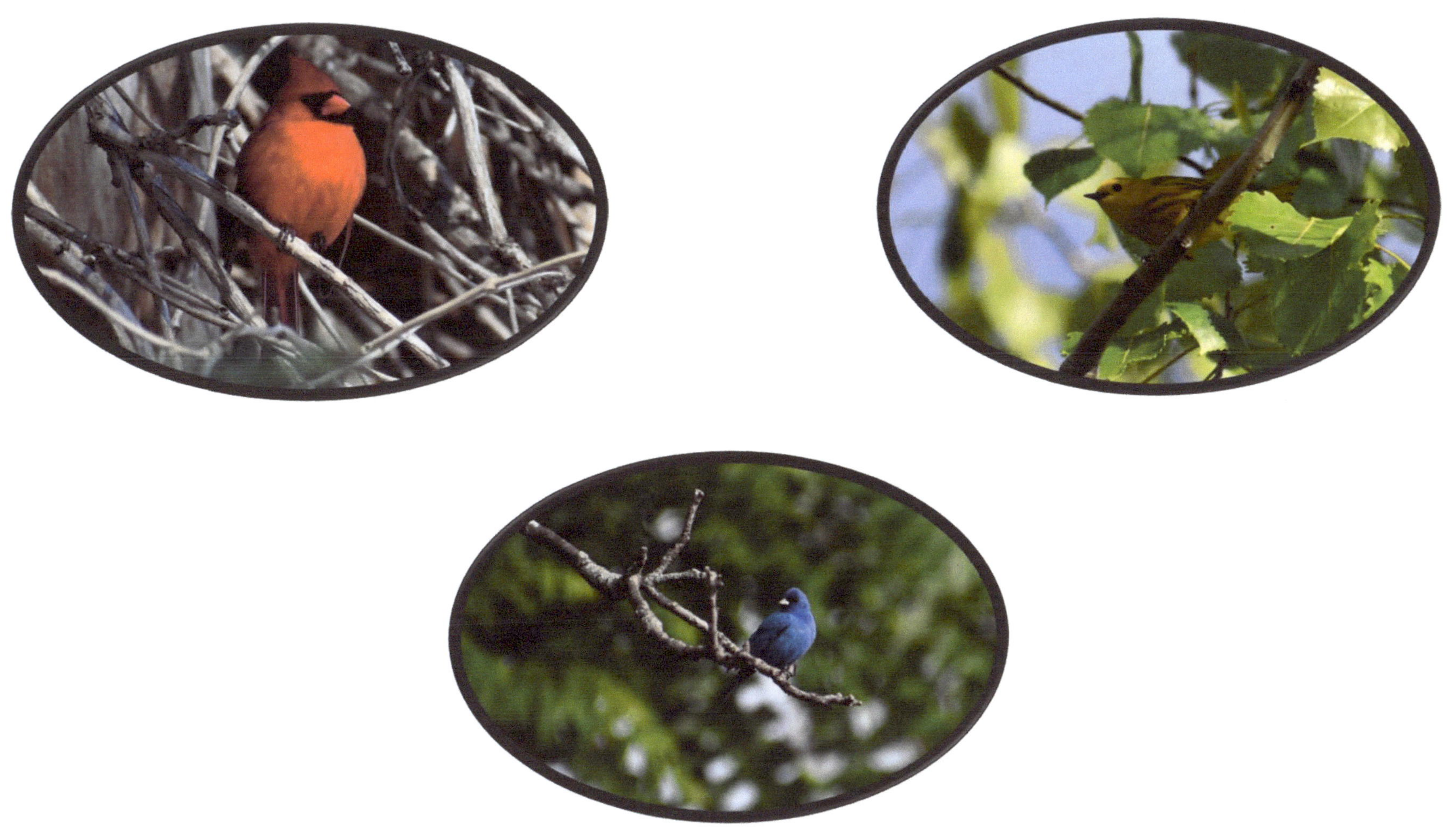

All colors start from just three.

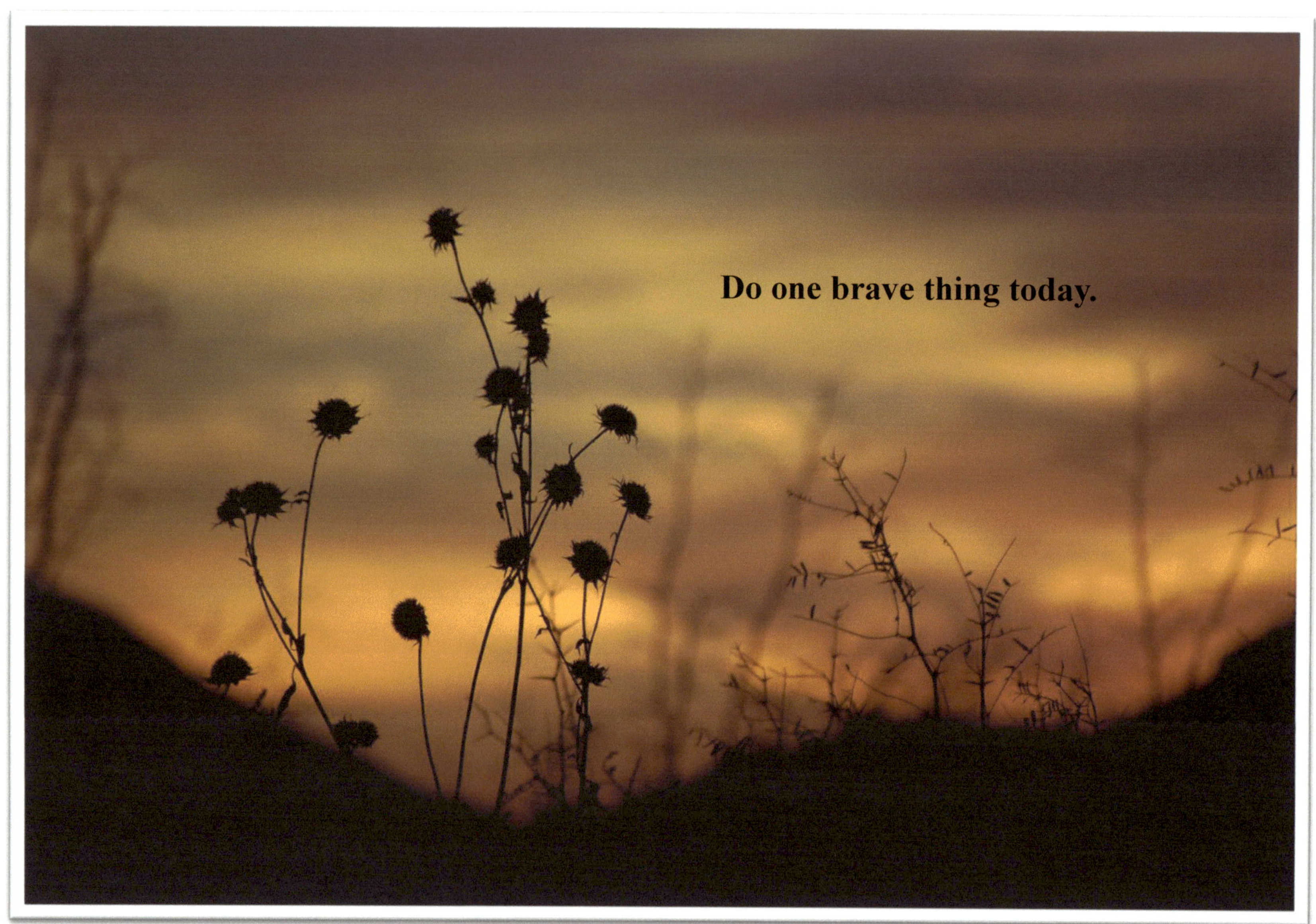
Do one brave thing today.

You'll never regret:

Loving too much

Taking vacations

Spending time with loved ones

Watching a baby sleep

Petting a dog

Listening to the night sounds

Forgiving

Learning something new

Trying something different

Spending time alone

Showing grace to another person

Helping a stranger

Learning your life's lessons

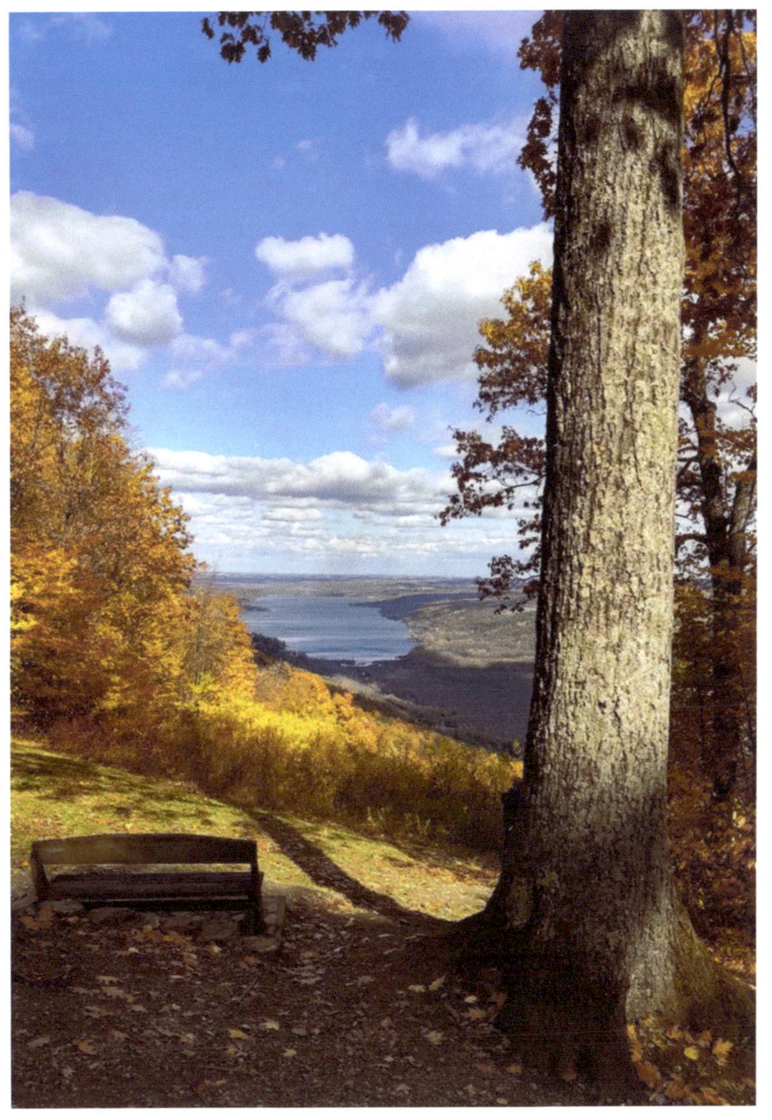

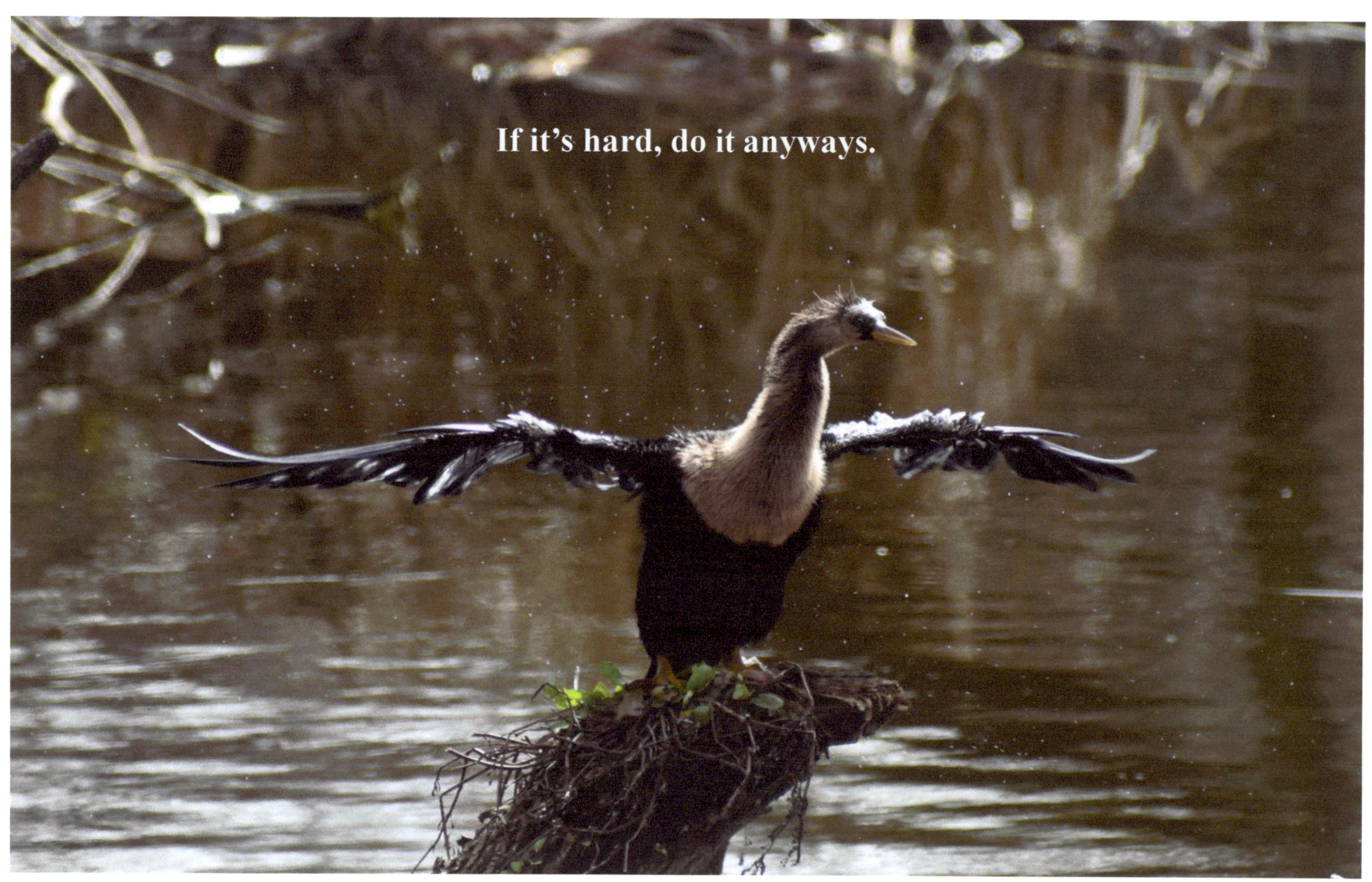If it's hard, do it anyways.

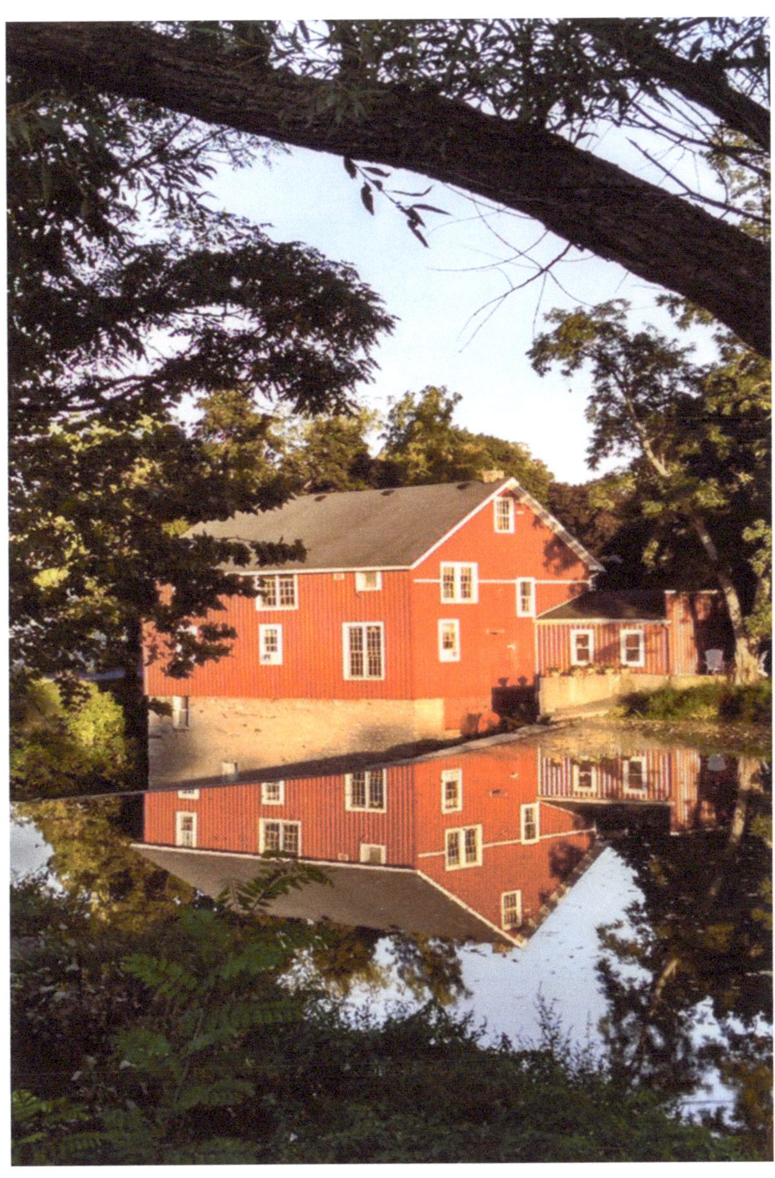

I will never forget a scene that played out one day a long time ago while I was at work. My husband had purchased a sports car for me for Christmas one year as a surprise. It was parked out front of the store where I was working, so I was able to keep an eye on it. A nice four-door sedan pulled up a couple cars down and an older couple got out. They were decked out in their finest Sunday best, looking very dapper. I was watching them as he stepped off the sidewalk and moved to the back of my car. He stopped, looked, and then proceeded around the other side and back to the sidewalk. Once in front of his lady he yelled "It's a Dodge Stealth!" She nodded and they continued on to their destination. Curiosity is alive and well at any age. Make sure you feed yours.

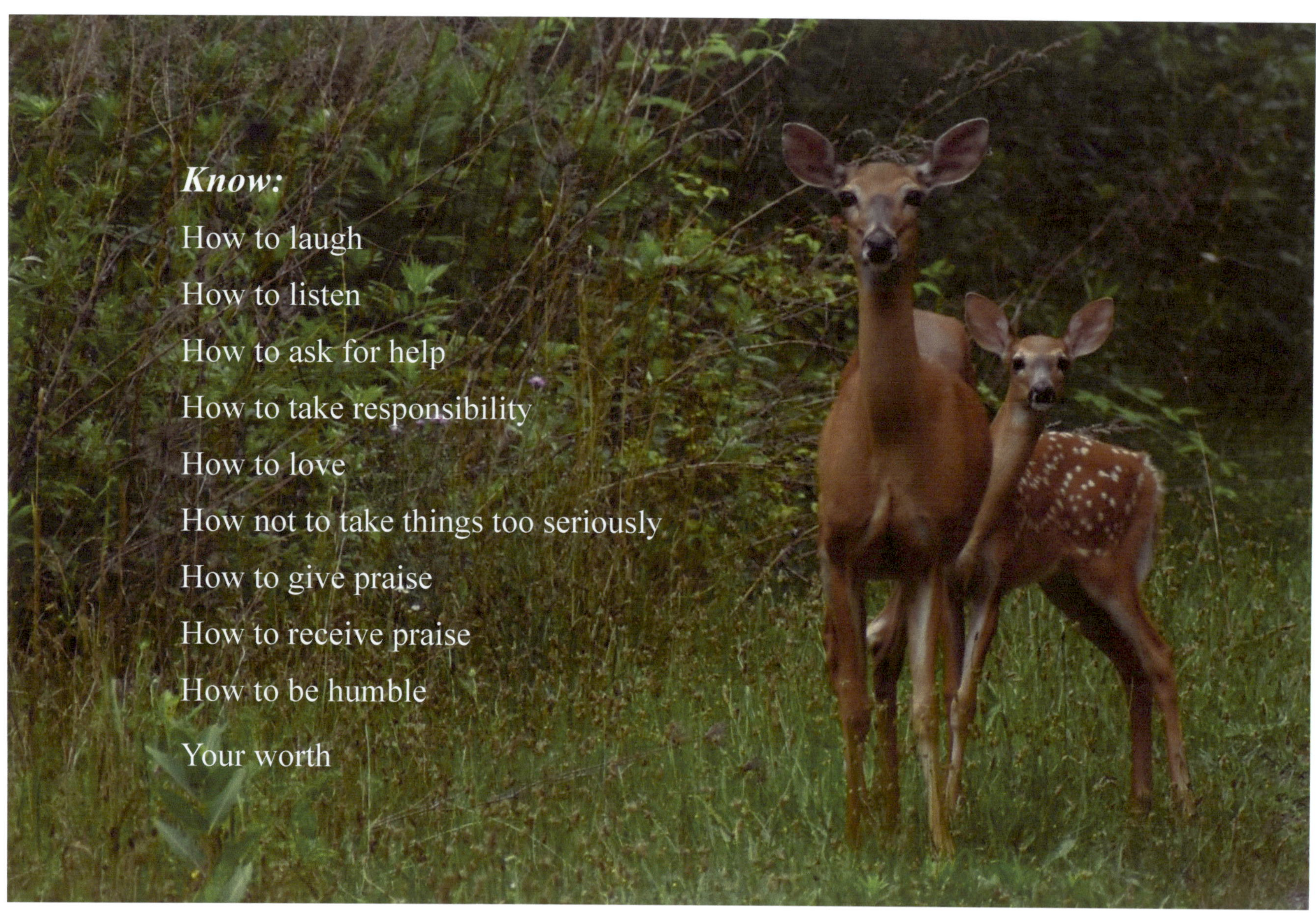

Know:

How to laugh

How to listen

How to ask for help

How to take responsibility

How to love

How not to take things too seriously

How to give praise

How to receive praise

How to be humble

Your worth

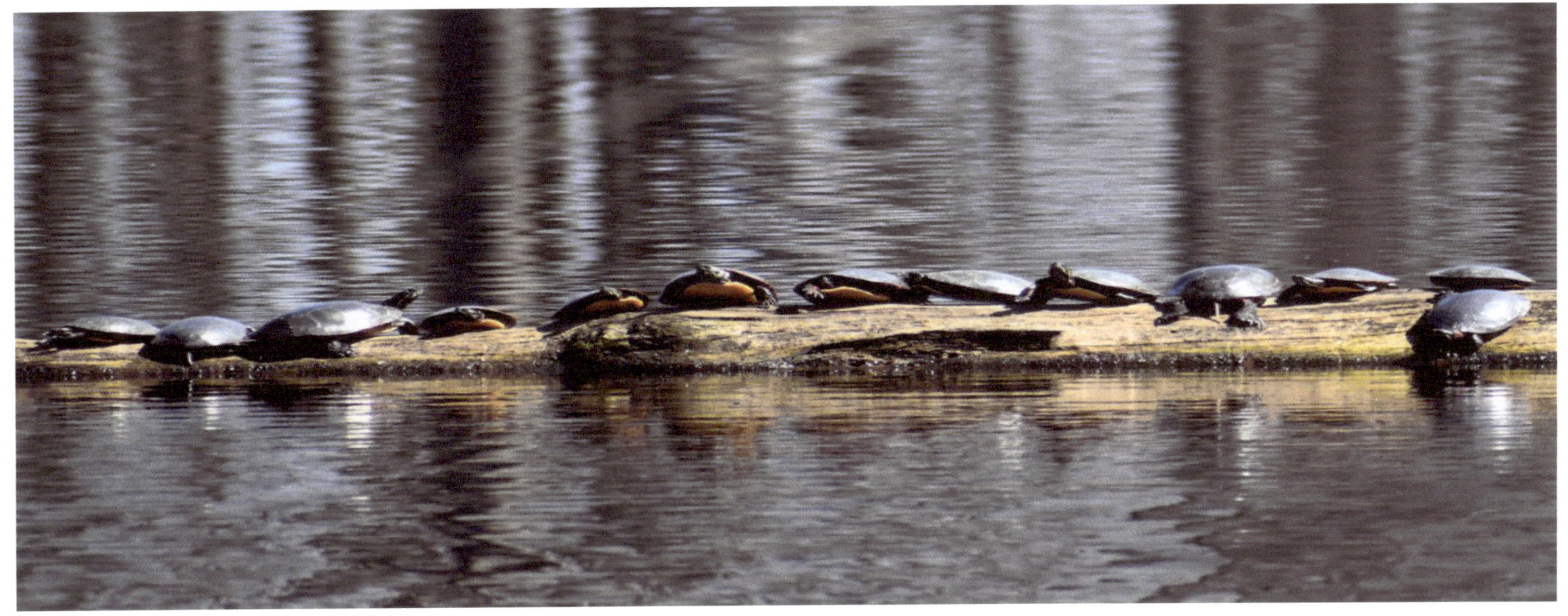

Just because we speak, think, and reason doesn't make us the king of all beasts. We can and have been outwitted by many a creature that doesn't speak our language.

When someone doesn't see what
they could do to help their situation,
it is up to you to let go and stop
trying to fix them. You cannot fight
for someone who is unwilling to
fight along with you.

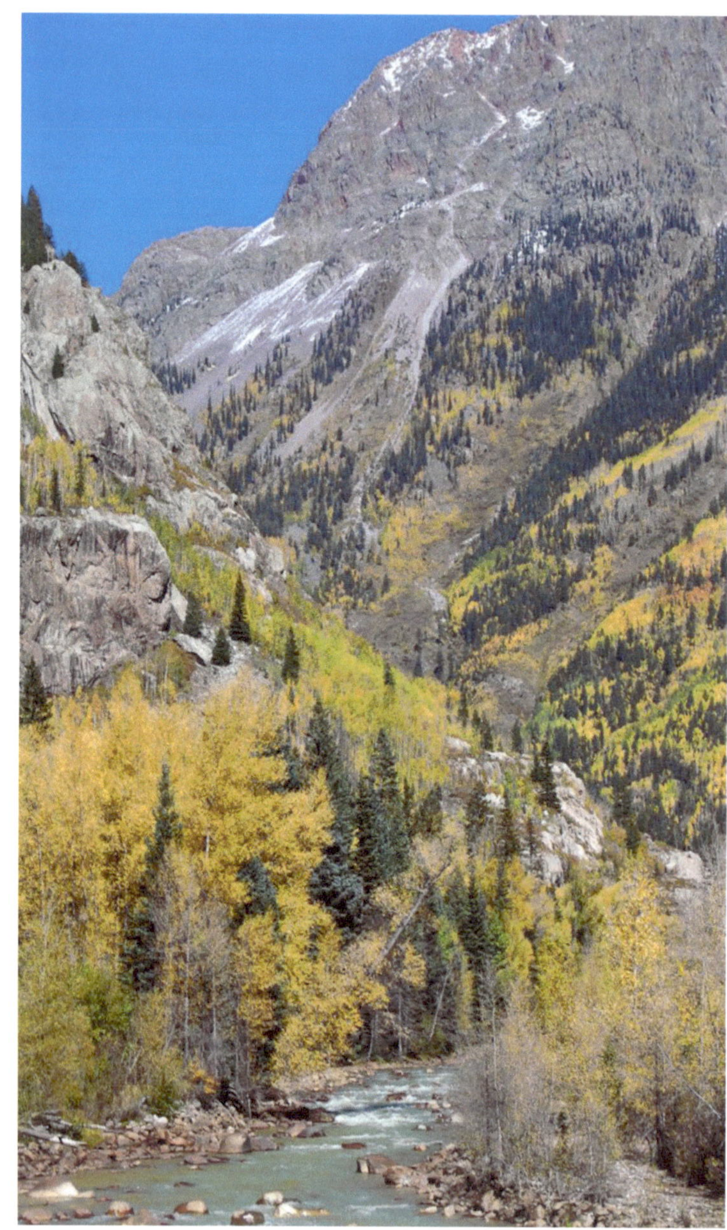

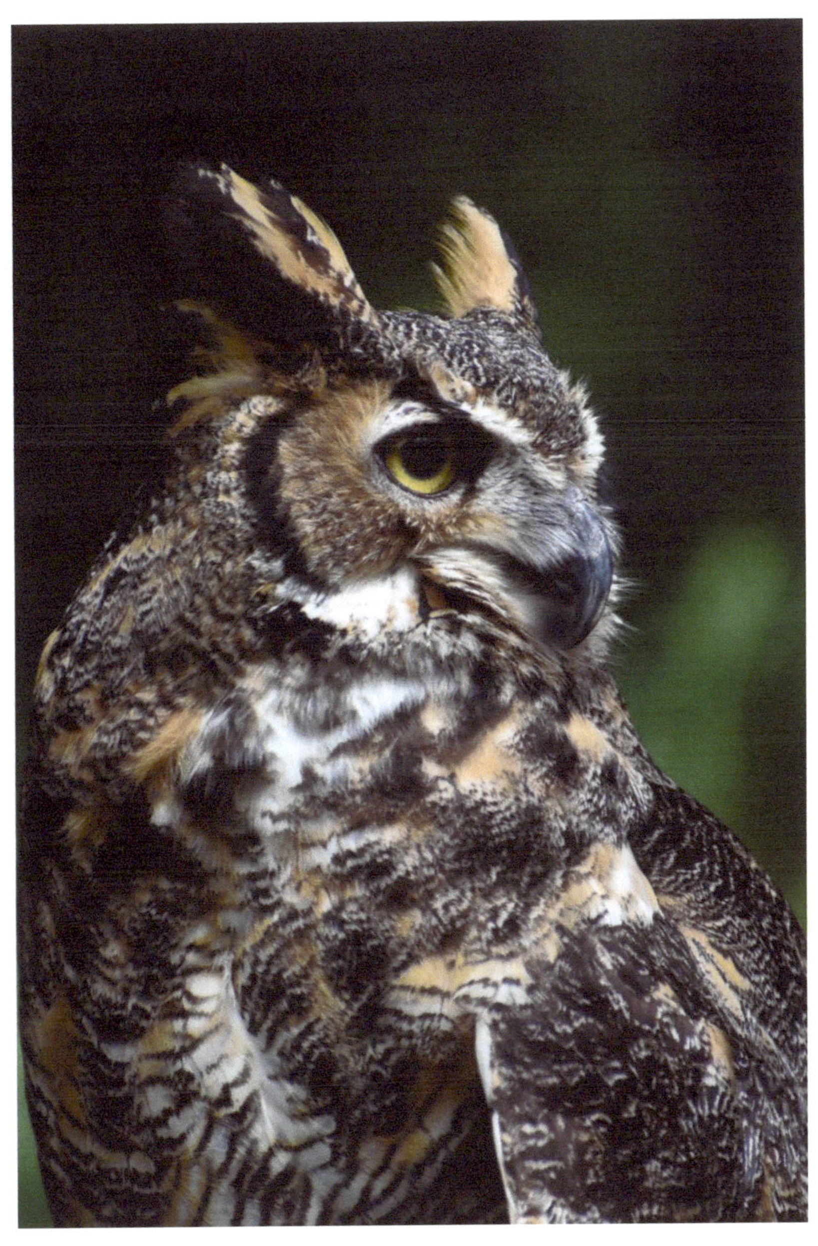

Be:

Honest

Grateful

Thankful

Brave

Hopeful

Faithful

Truthful

Helpful

Confident

Loving

Kind

Happy with who you are

Make sure you make enough memories to last you into old age.

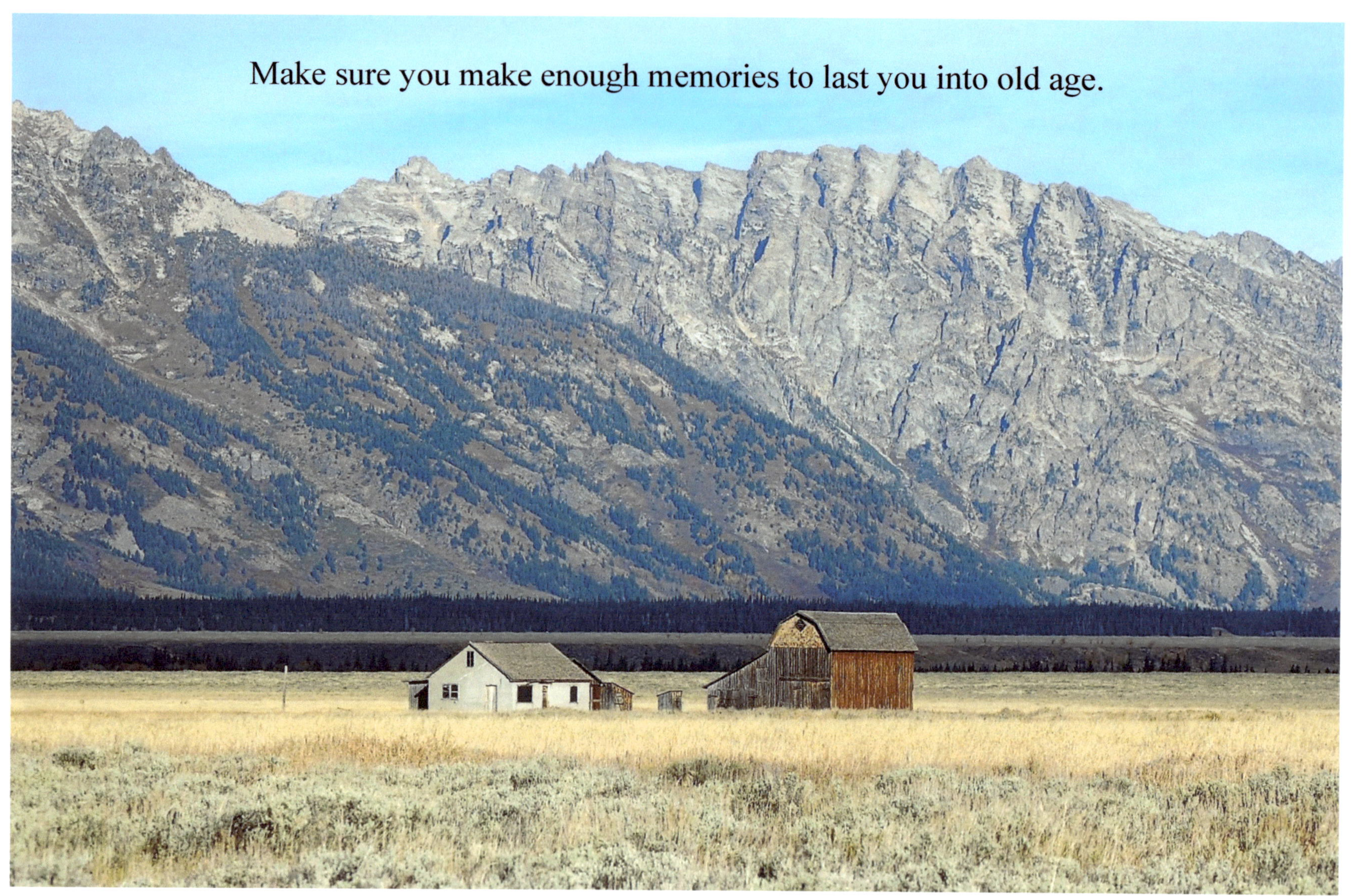

When you mention turkey vultures, most people think of an ugly dirty bird. Something that creeps them out because it feeds on death.

Let me tell you a little about these birds. First, they are one of the only species of birds that actually use their sense of smell. They have a territory that they canvass from the air, and when they smell decay, they start to circle. This is to alert the other vultures that dinner is below. Soon several birds will converge to feed. By doing this, all of them get fed—not just one. They work together for the good of all.

The lesson is simple; it is not "survival of the fitness" or the selfish, but survival of the selfless.

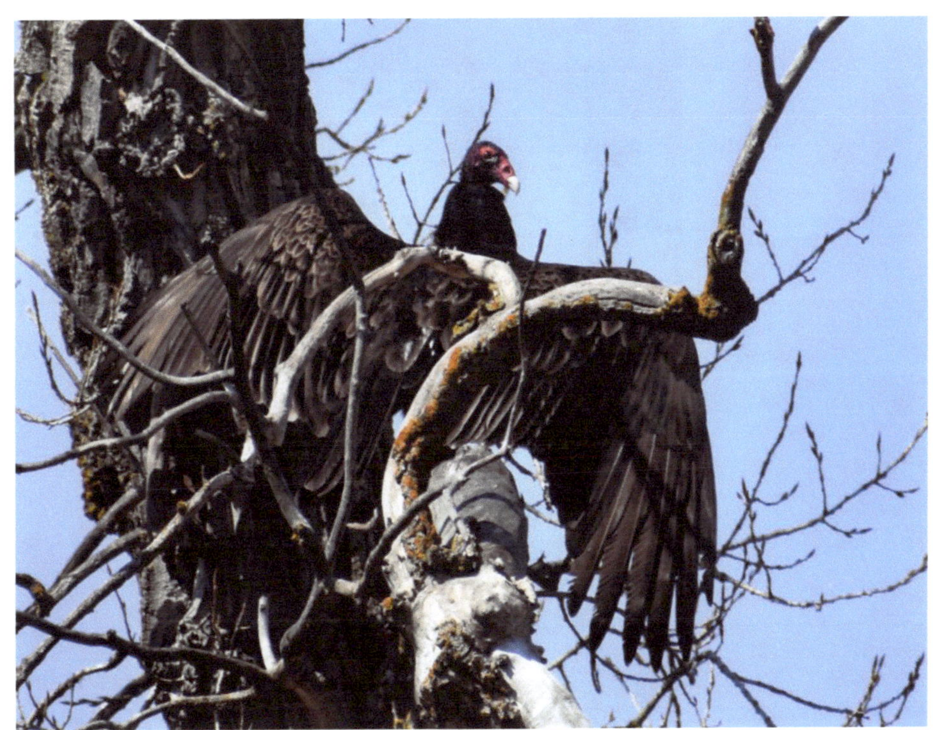

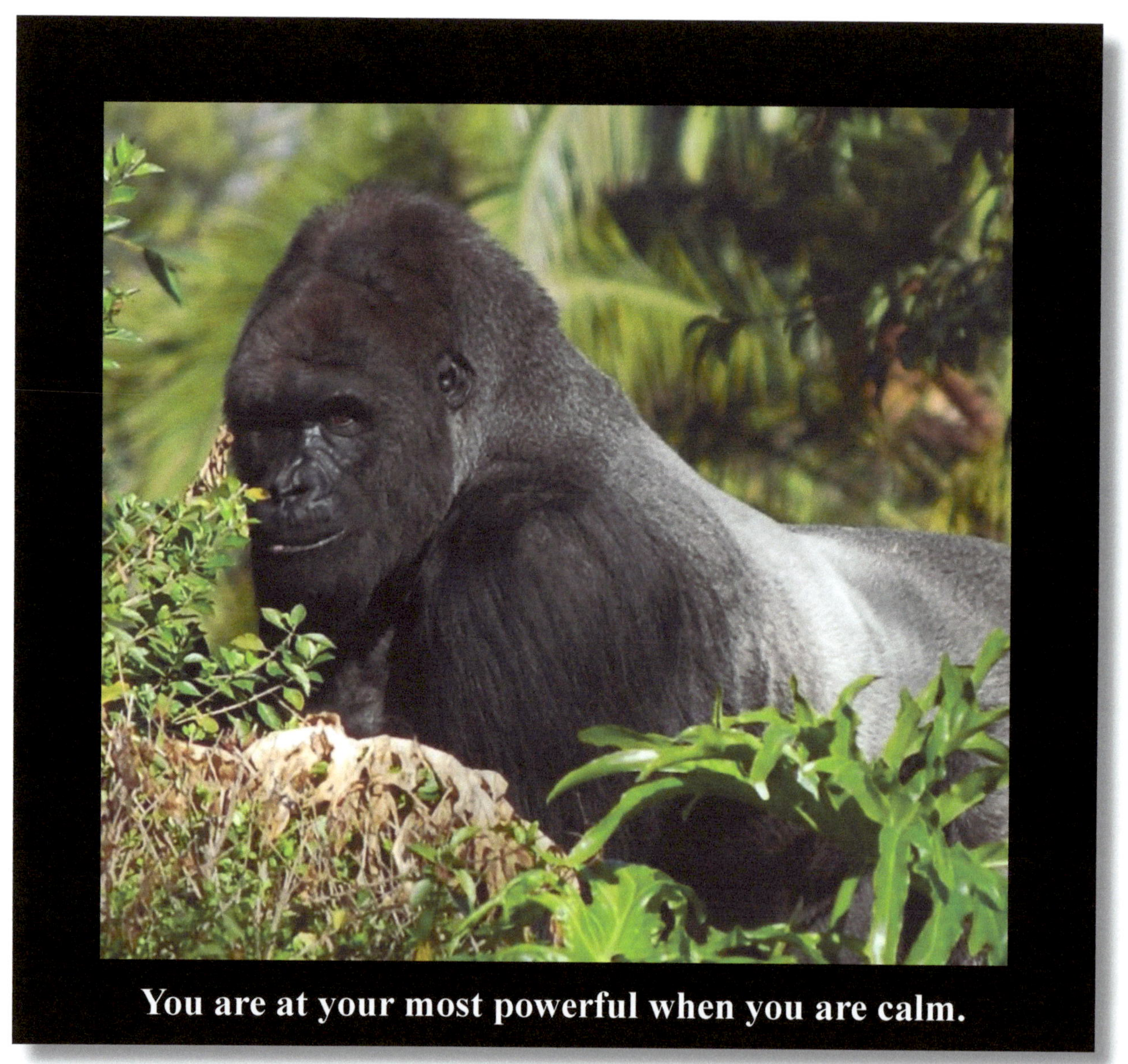

You are at your most powerful when you are calm.

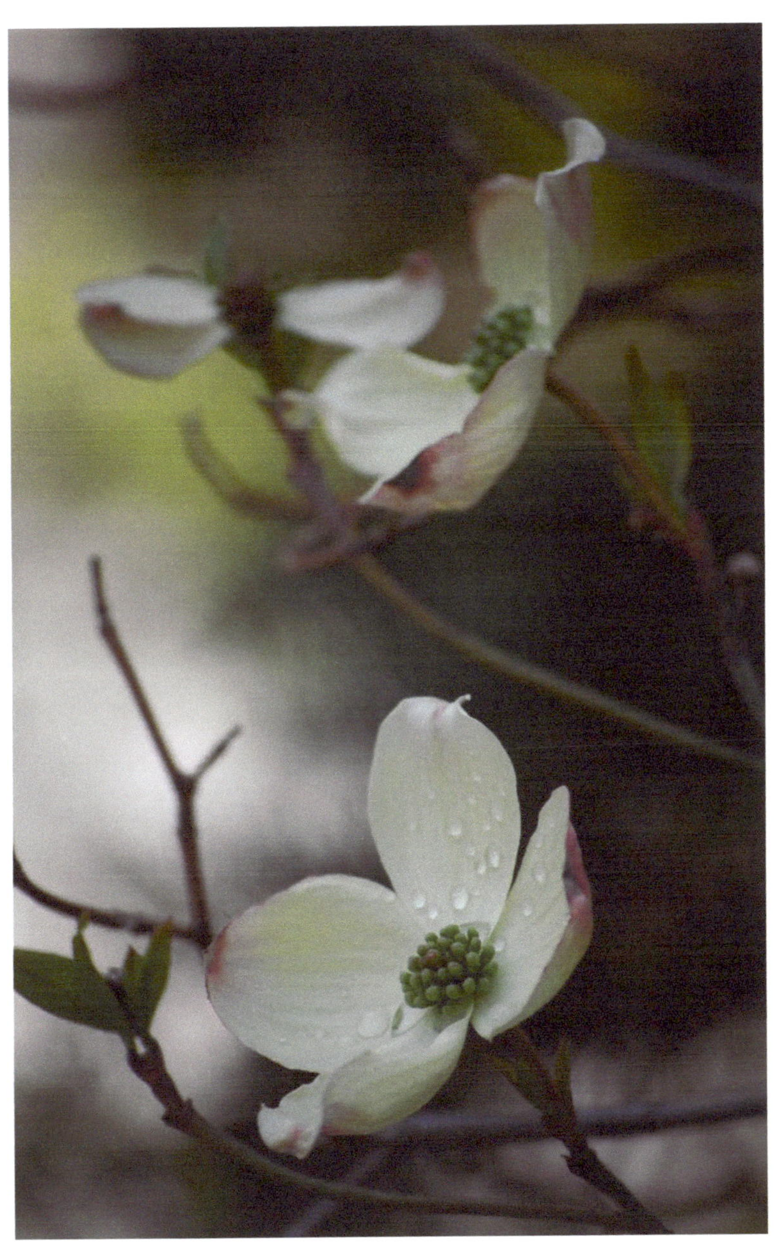

Always remember to:

Love with your whole heart

Forgive with your whole heart

Look for the next right thing to do

Help someone without looking for thanks or praise

Be curious

Listen with your whole heart

Respect your elders

Never stop learning

Don't look too close.

The bum slumped on the street corner.

Don't look too close.

He may be a war vet that never was able to process the fact that six of his best friends were blown to bits by an IED and he lived.

The child who is having a meltdown in an aisle at Walmart.

Don't look too close.

He may be one of millions of children suffering from Autism.

The bully picking on the kid on the playground.

Don't look too close.

You may see that this child is only doing to others what has been done to him his whole young life.

The old man sitting alone nursing a beer.

Don't look too close.

You may see he has nothing to go home to because his wife of 60 years is in a nursing home, and she doesn't know him anymore.

The cranky old lady that lives next door that's grass is too long.

Don't look too close.

You may see someone that cannot afford to hire anyone, and is too embarrassed or proud to just ask for help.

The man standing in the middle of the grocery store in everyone's way.

Don't look to close.

You may see someone that is desperately trying to get everything on the list his sick wife made so he can get home to her.

The young man strung out in the alley unable to stand.

Don't look to close.

You may see someone that was abused so badly as a child that no amount of counselling can convince him he is worth anything.

Things aren't always what they seem to be. It only takes a moment to look at someone with empathy and compassion. To realize that what we thought we saw wasn't what was really there at all.

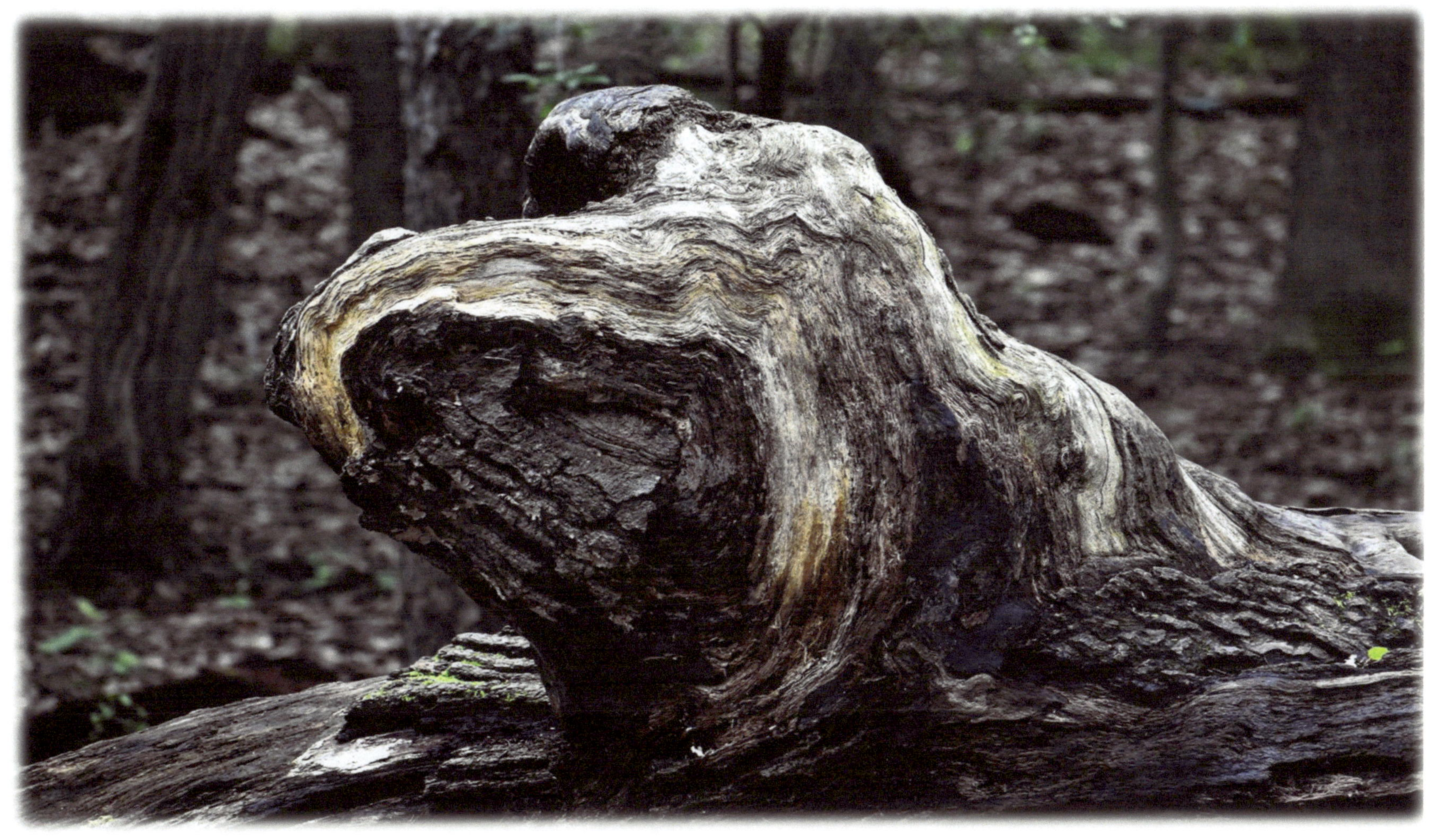

Whether it is a mountain or a mole hill depends on how you look at it.

Be who you were meant to be.

Do what you were meant to do.

Say what you were meant to say.

Find your purpose.

And in the end if you were only able
to help one other person, you did
good.

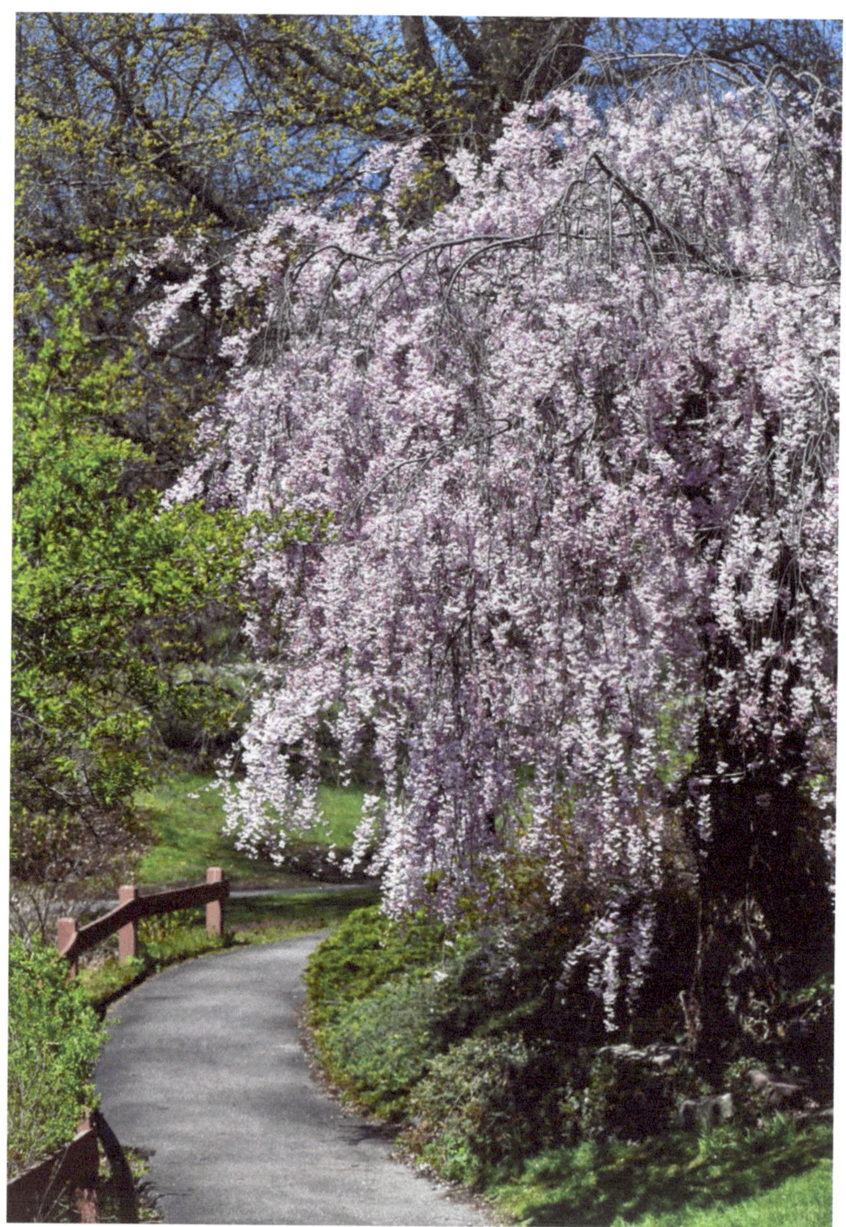

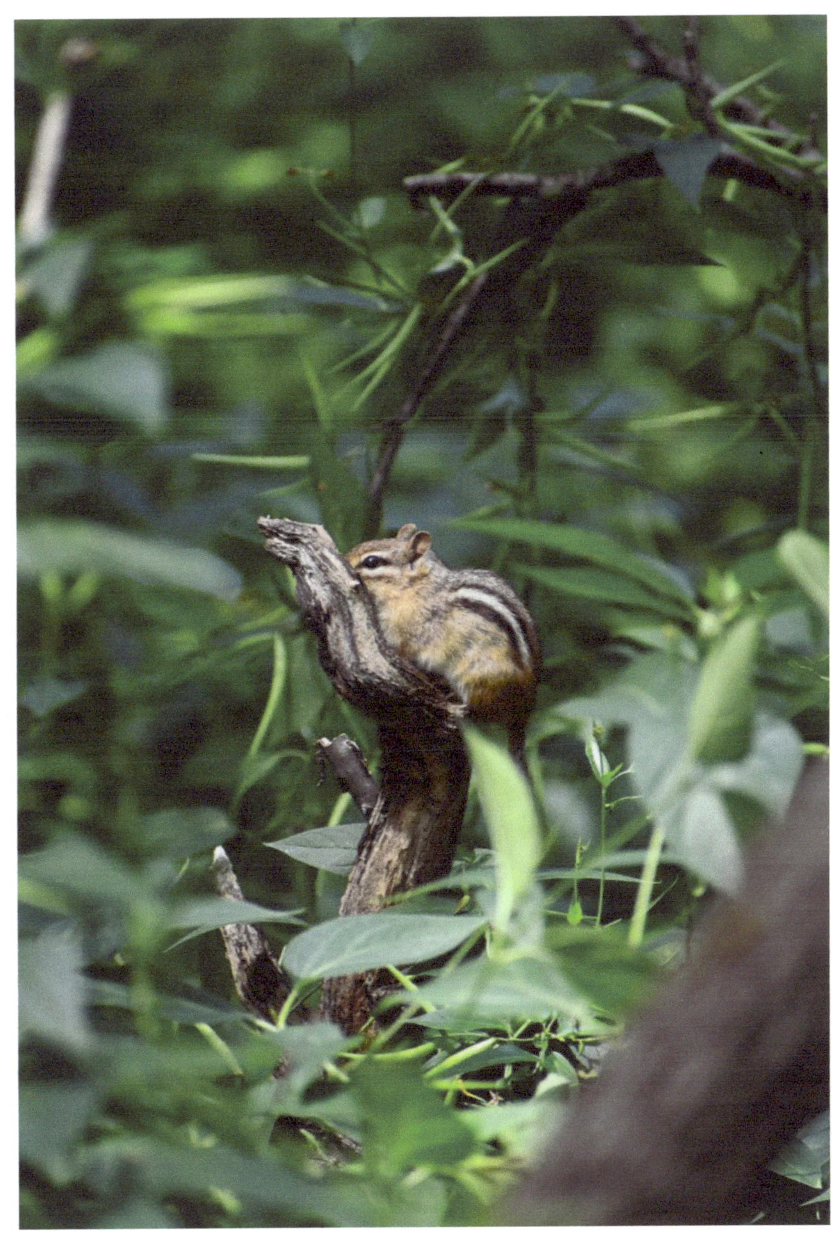

Throw your regrets, your worries, your guilt, and your troublesome thoughts and memories into the trash not the recycle bin.

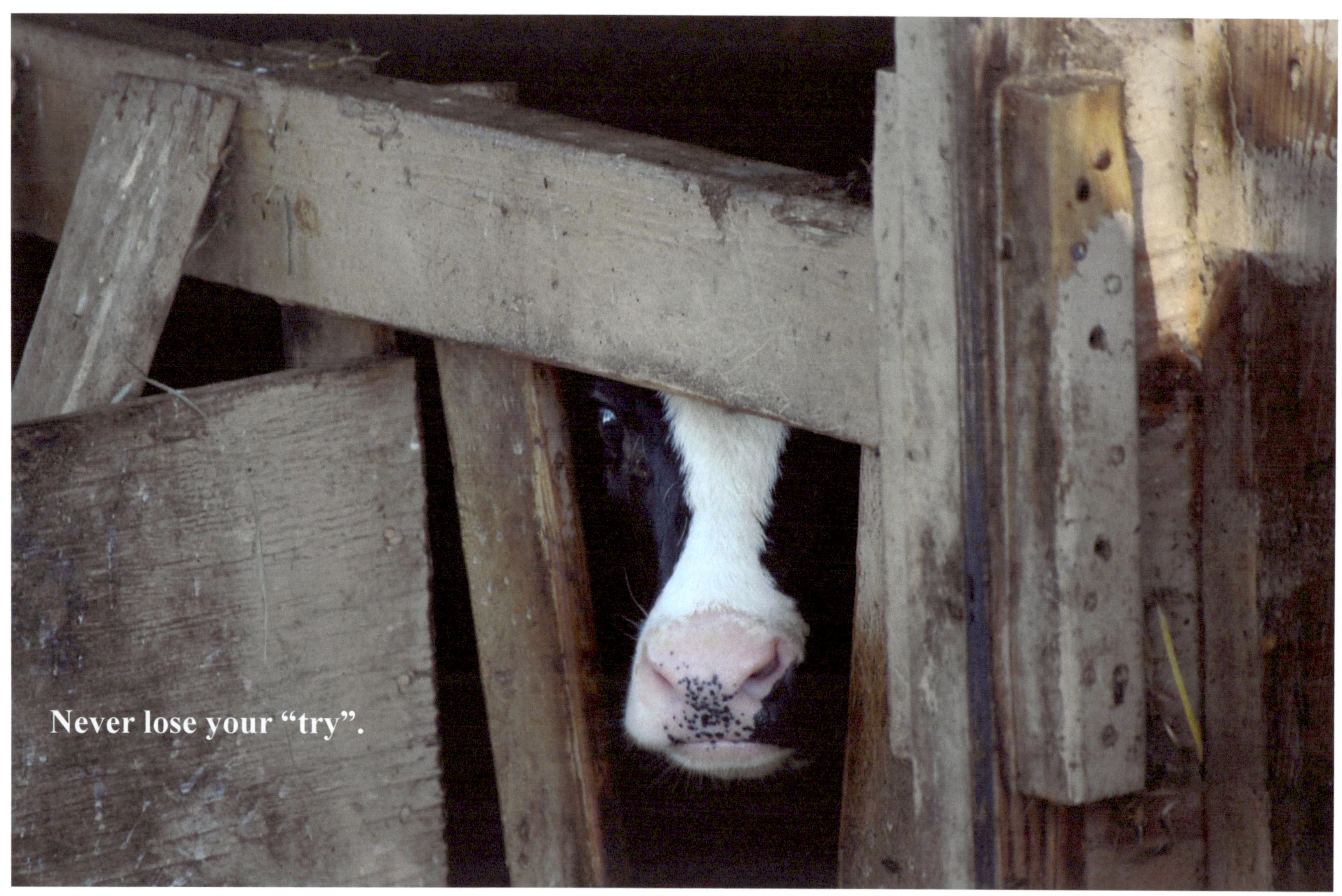

Never lose your "try".

It is ridiculous to drive like there is
someone in your lane as you cross over
the top of a hill. Life shouldn't be lived
like that either.

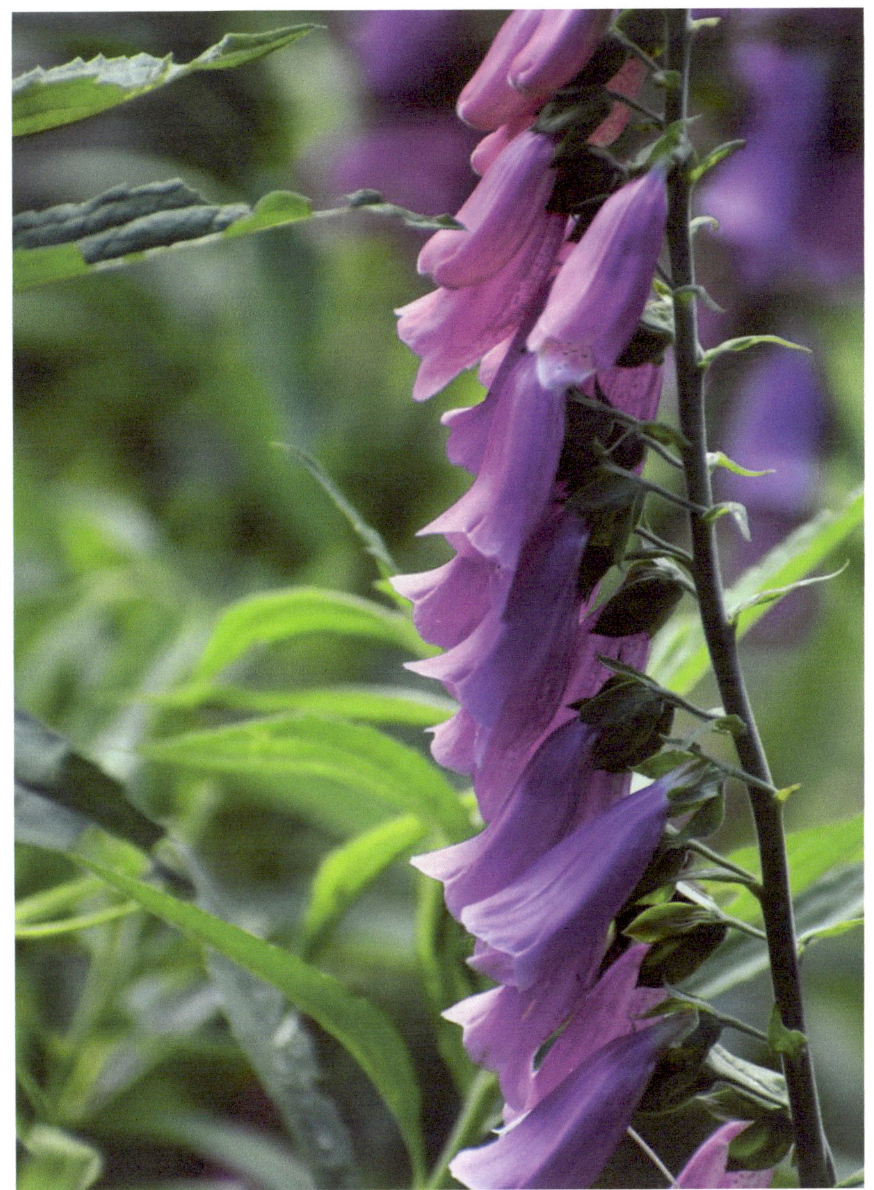

Don't wait to get motivated before you begin to do something. Don't wait until you are ready to do it. Do it, and you will be ready. Don't wait for the circumstances to be right. Some people are procrastinators and always say that they will wait until later to do something. Others are perfectionists and wait for the conditions to be perfect before they do something. Instead of being a procrastinator or perfectionist you should *just do it*. You may not be able to always count on the circumstances, but you can always count on your actions.

You have the power of choice, so make the choice to do it.

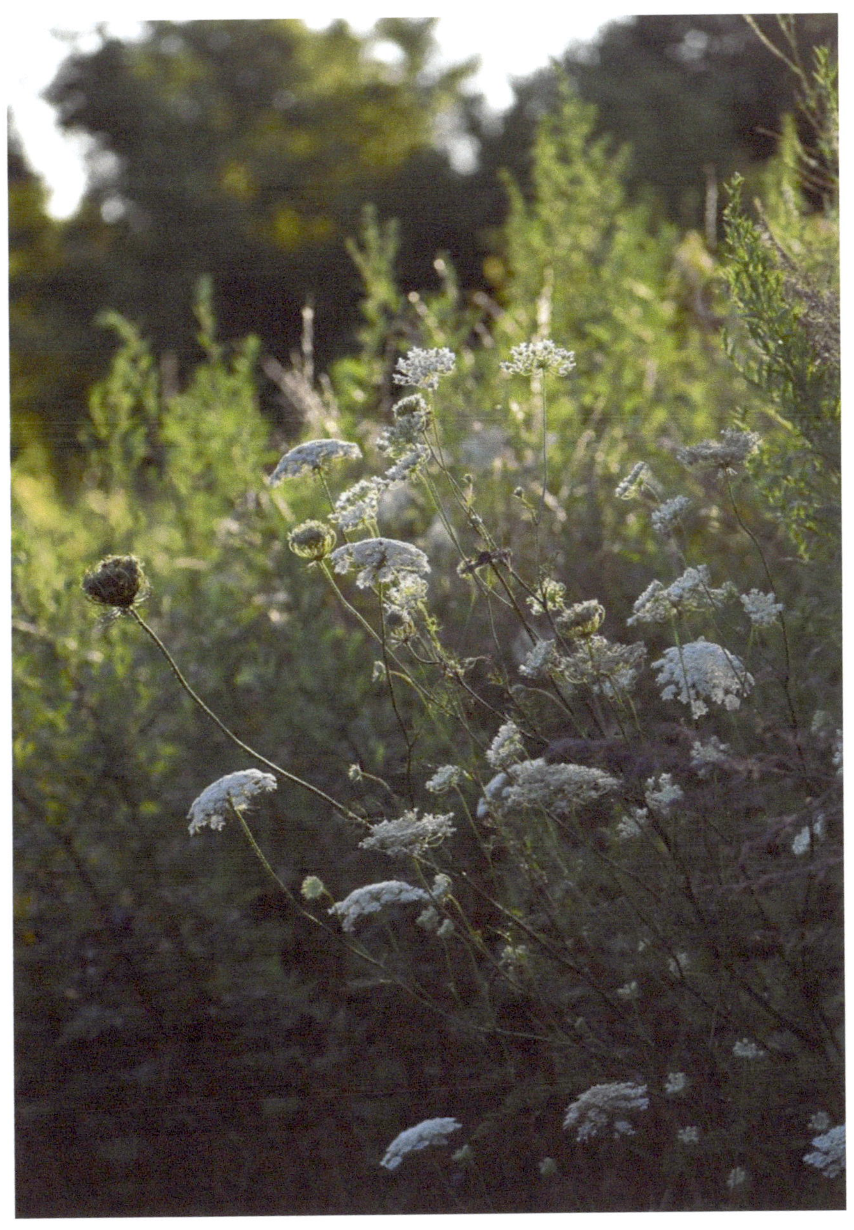

Life is like a bicycle ride; there is a beginning and an end. How difficult you make the middle depends on what gear you're in.

Be your own disco ball.

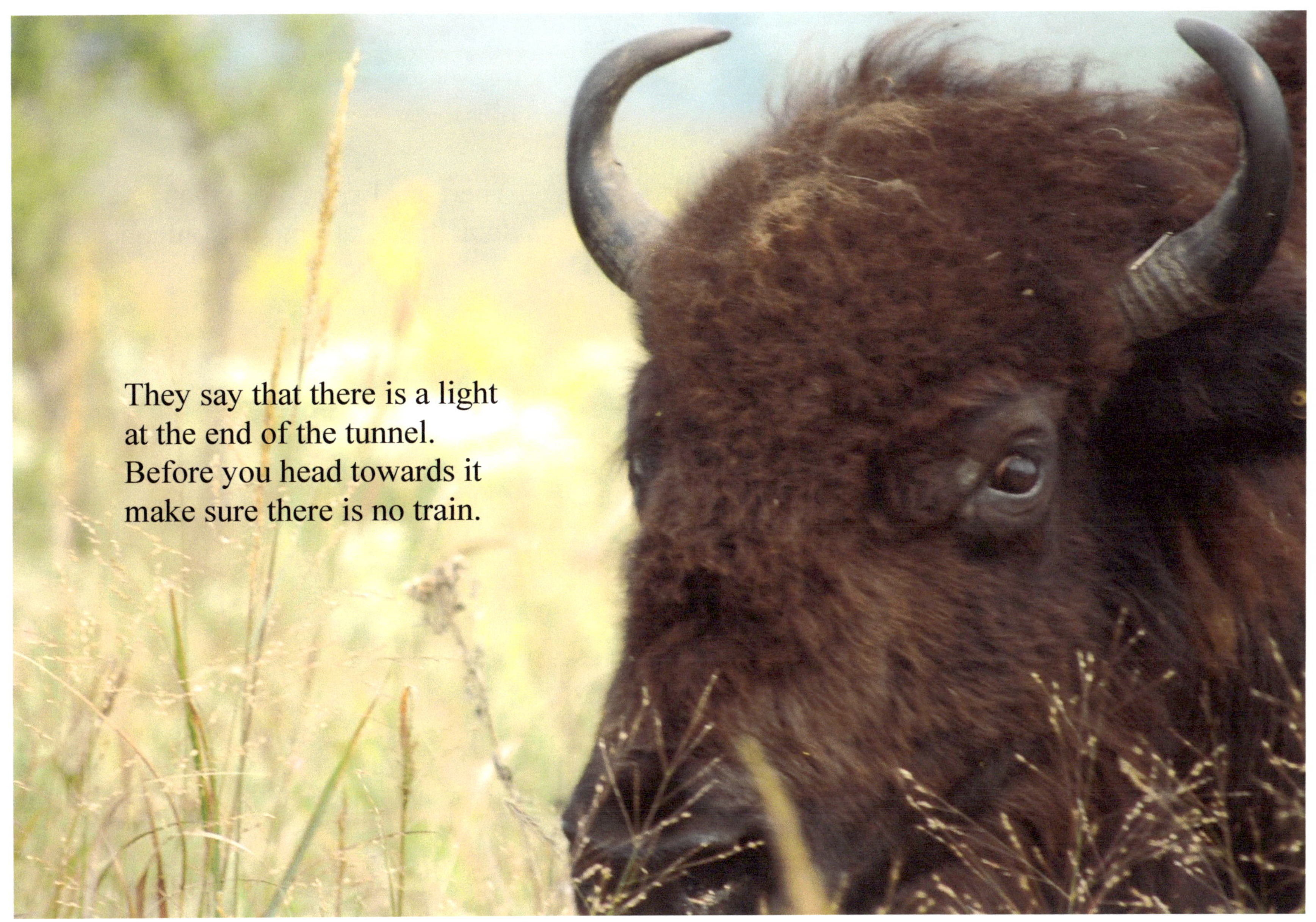

They say that there is a light
at the end of the tunnel.
Before you head towards it
make sure there is no train.

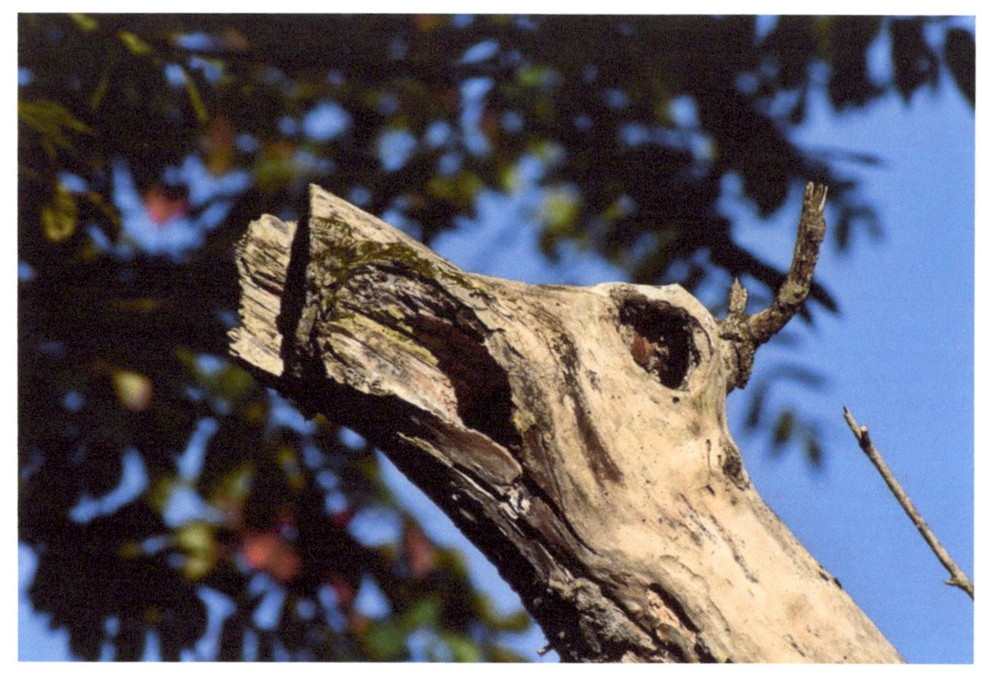

There is always more than one way to look at something, or someone.

You are exactly who you perceive yourself to be. Only you can change your perception of yourself.

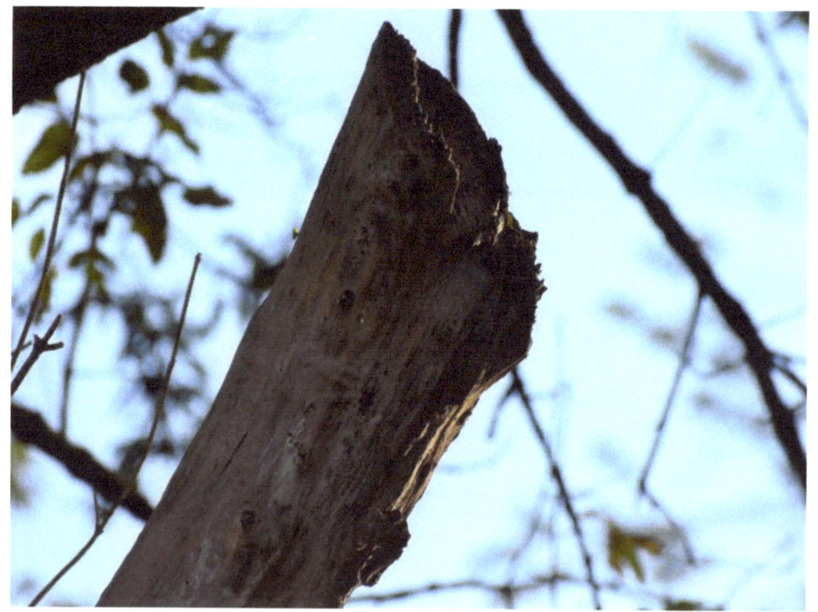

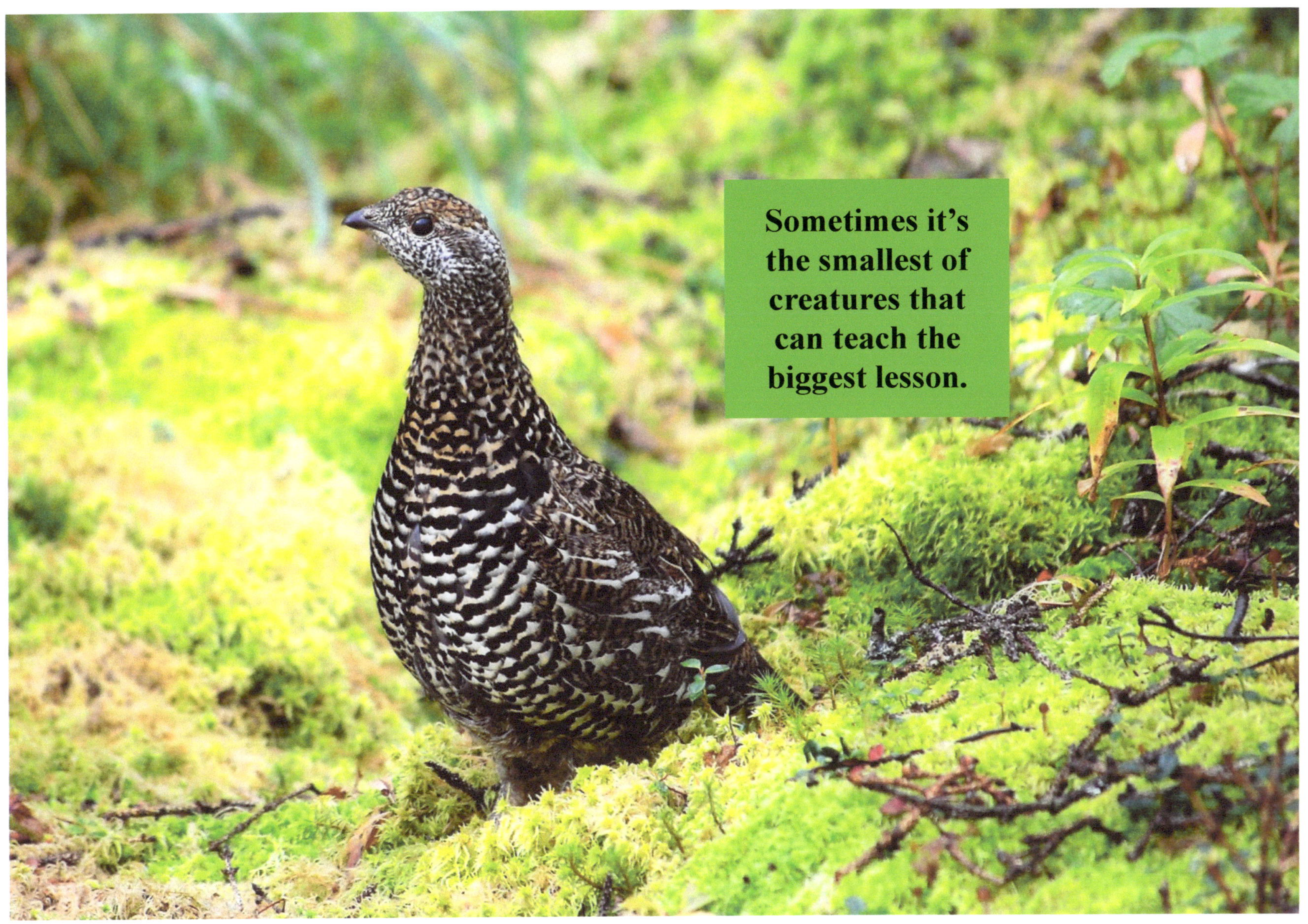
Sometimes it's
the smallest of
creatures that
can teach the
biggest lesson.

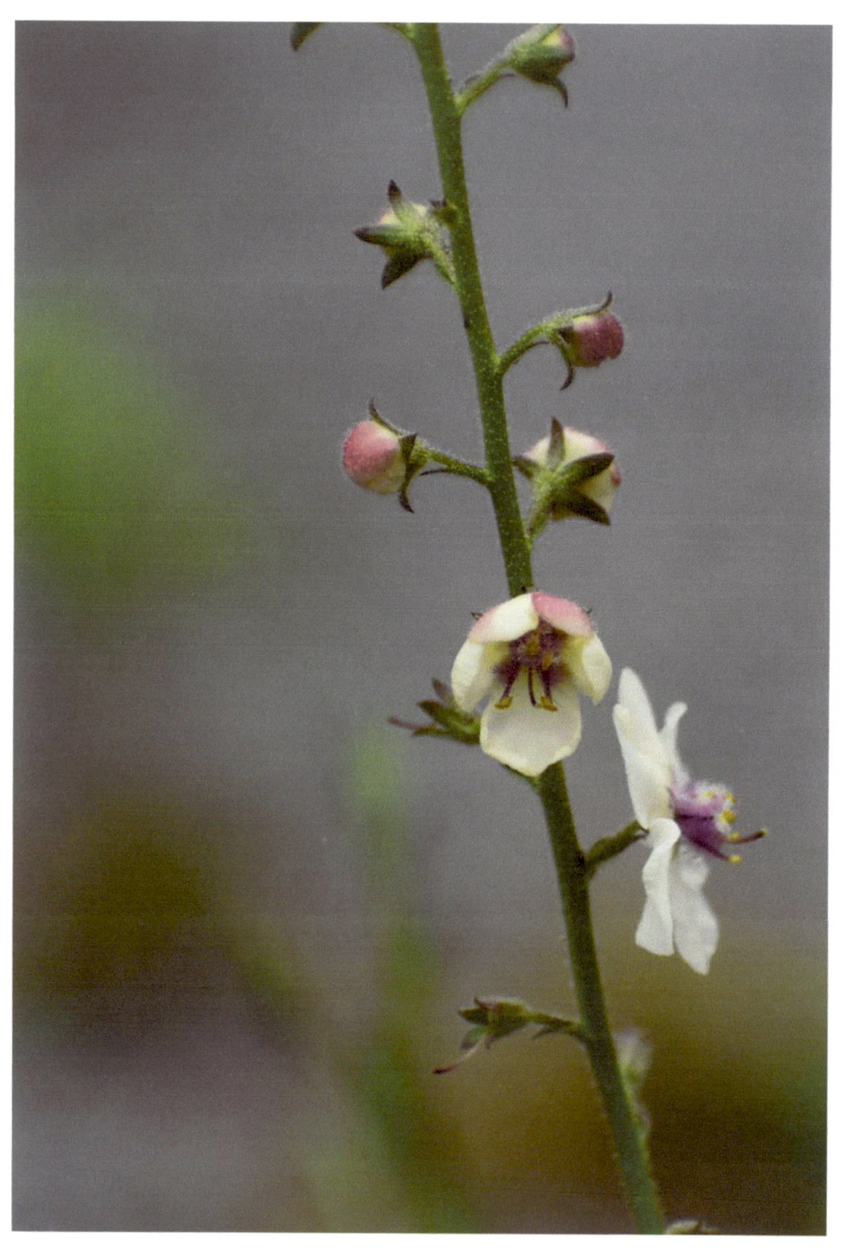

You can talk yourself into or out of
anything … choose wisely.

The garbage:

When we were first married, oh so many years ago, my hubby told me this: If you need me to help out, you will have to tell me what to do; I'm not very good at seeing what needs to be done.

He walked by a bag of garbage three times and didn't take it out. (Garbage is his thing, not mine; I have enough). Now, I could have called him back downstairs and asked him to take care of it, but I didn't.

The reason is simple. When someone tells you something honestly and from the heart, take it as their truth. We all have our weaknesses. We all have our strengths. I would rather be grateful for him—the entire being, with all his faults—than to be without him. So, I took out the trash. And smiled that God blessed me with him.

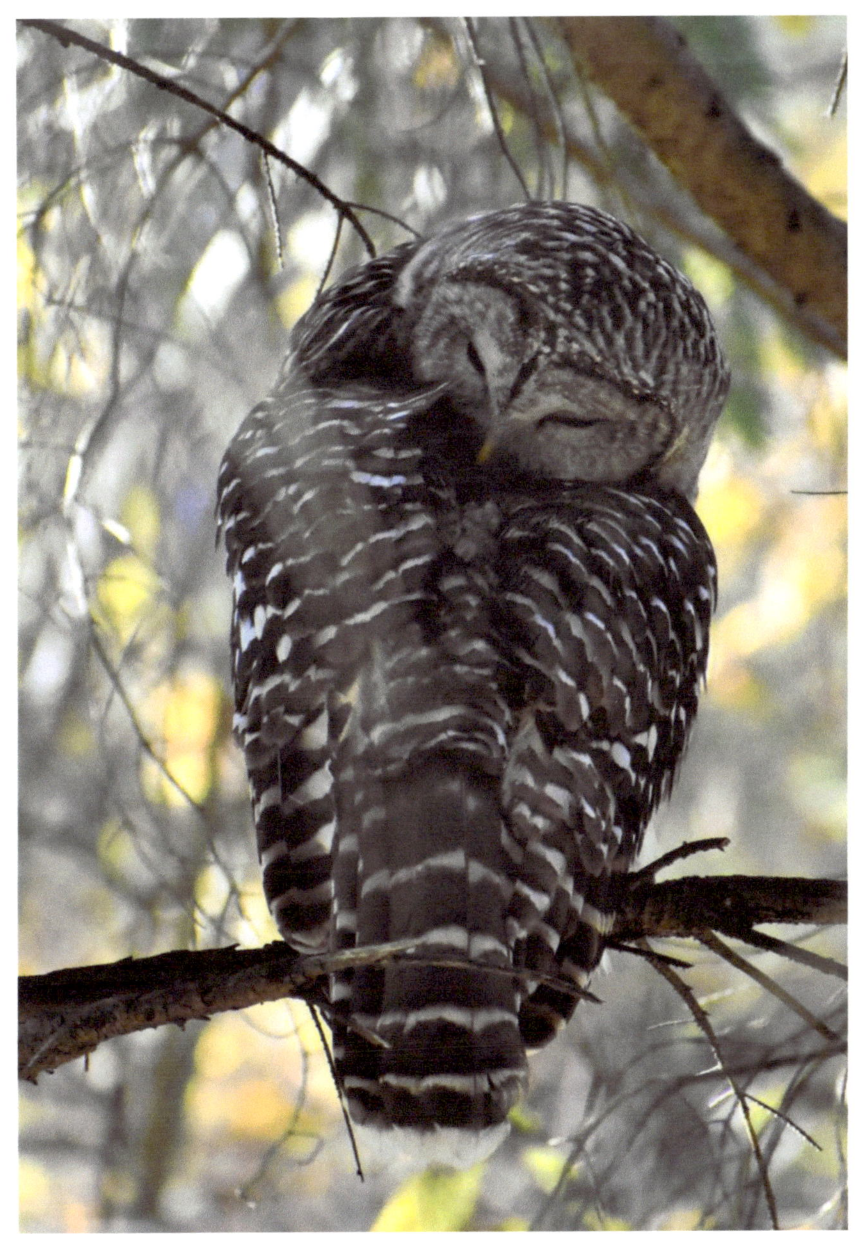

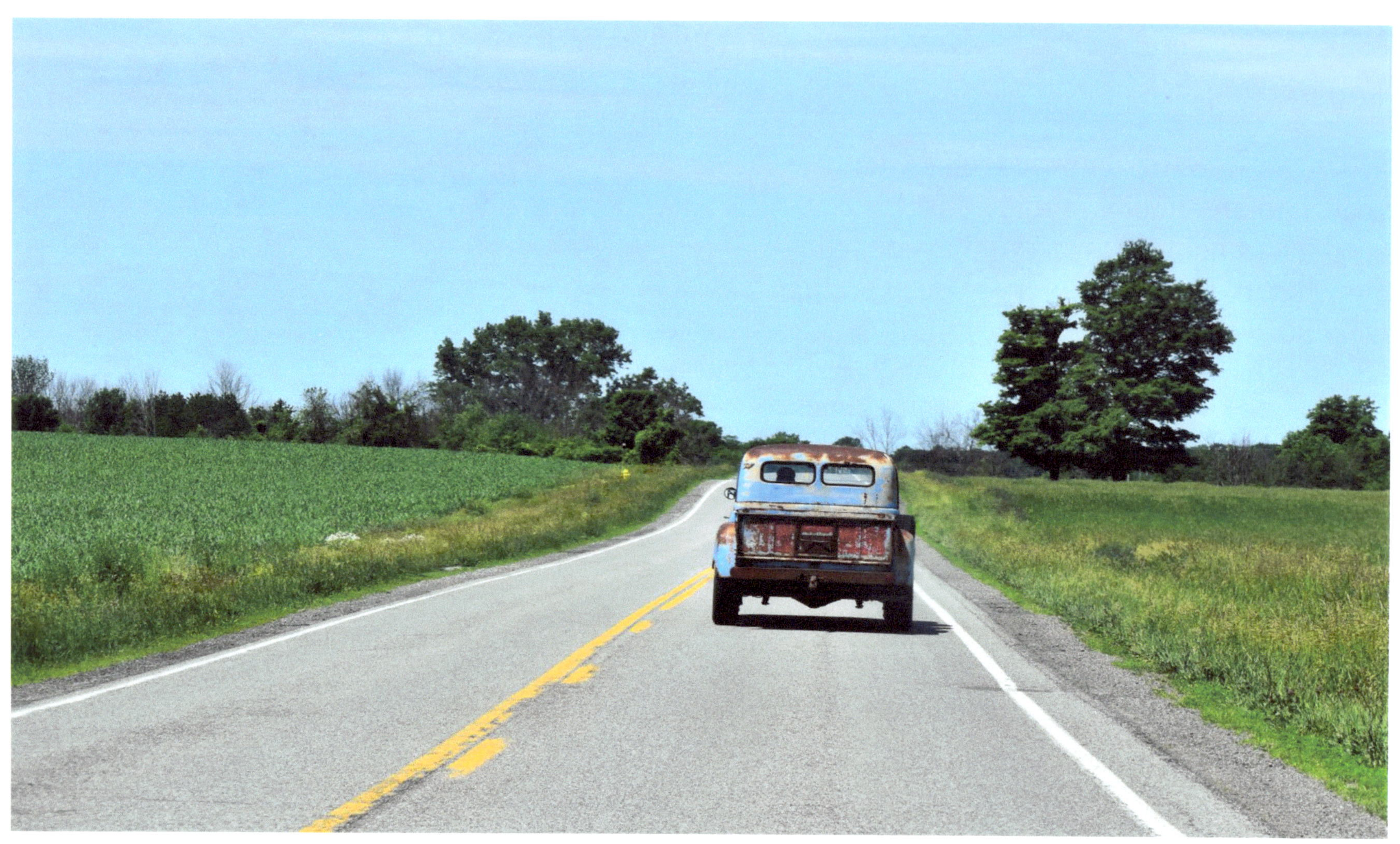

When your mind is rushing like a six-lane highway take the time to exit off onto a two-lane road. Breathe, relax, and enjoy the view. Let your mind wonder around the bends in the road. Until you can put everything in the rear-view mirror at least for a little while.

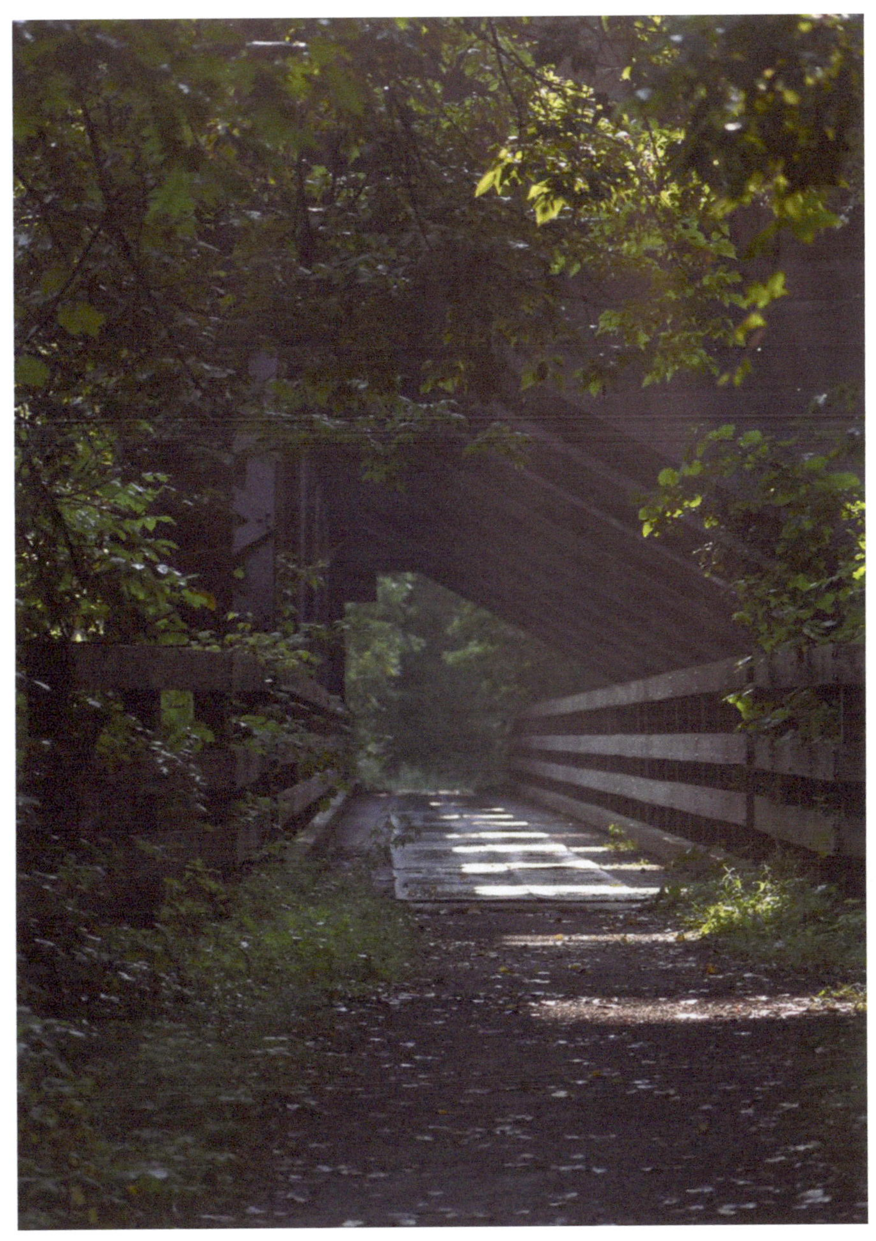

The sooner you realize that trying to change someone's opinion is as impossible as trying to stop Niagara Falls the happier you will be.

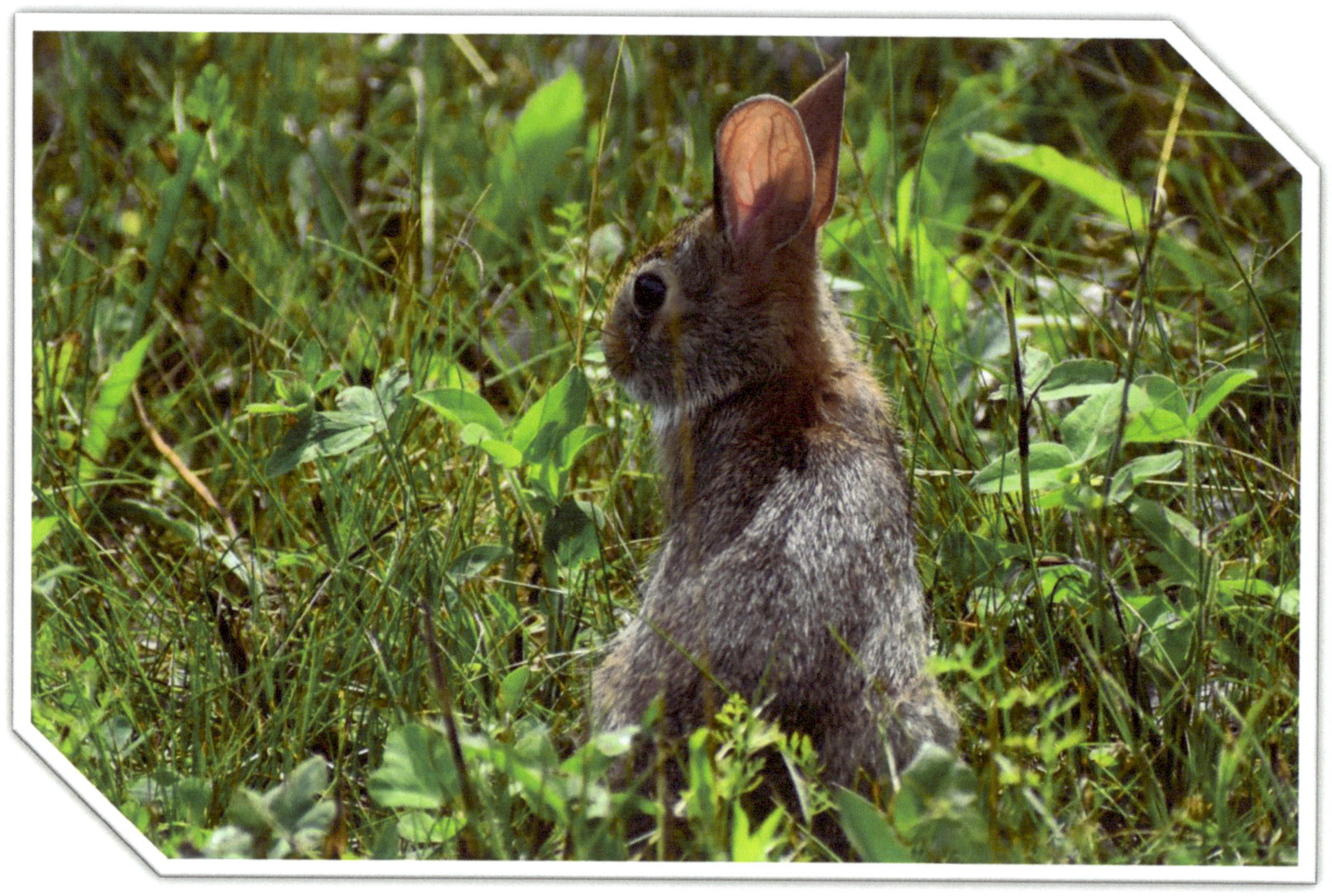

When dealing with a difficult situation, go into it with two things: faith and an exit strategy.

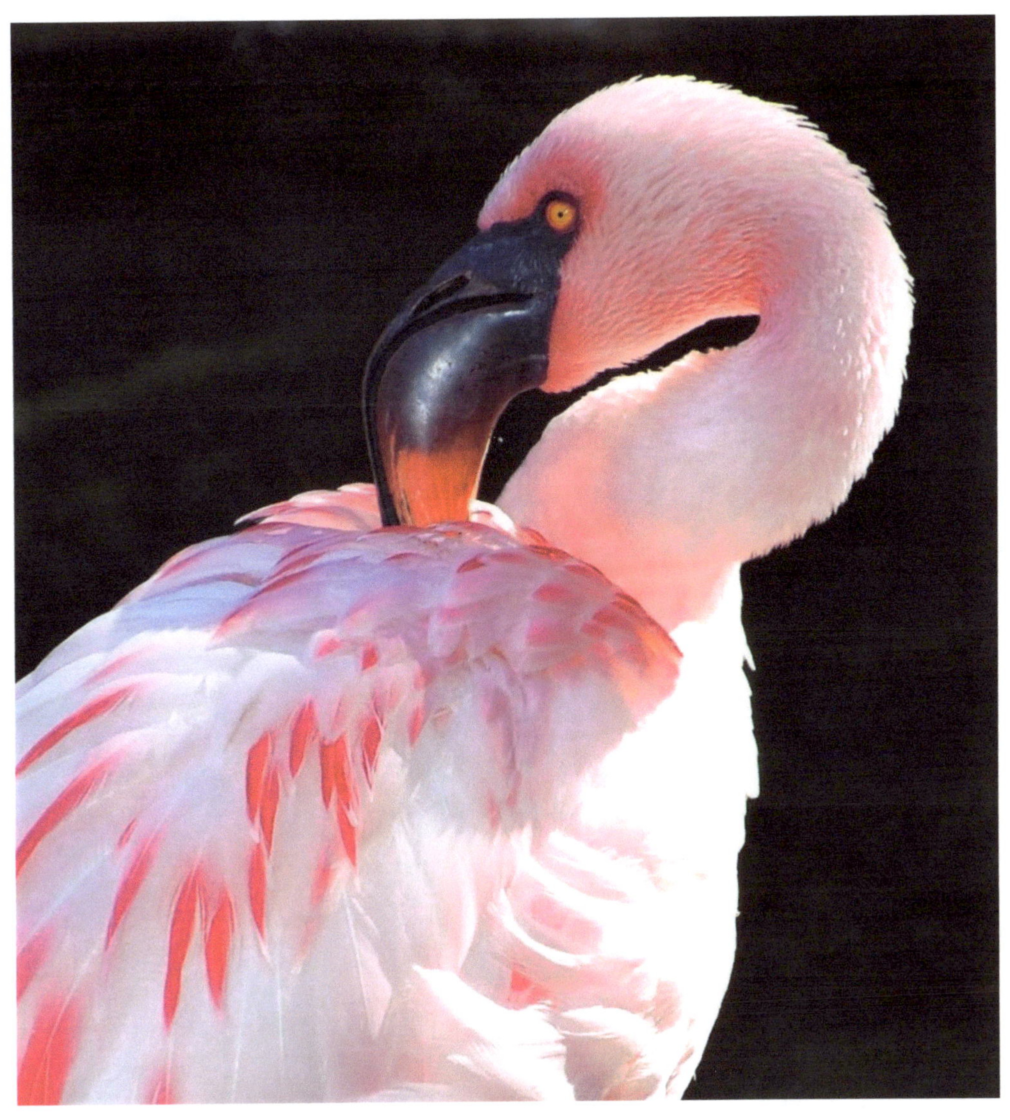

Every now and then you
need to just be fancy.

We all have:

Burdens

Curiosity

Creativity

Sorrow

Joy

Patience

The ability to love

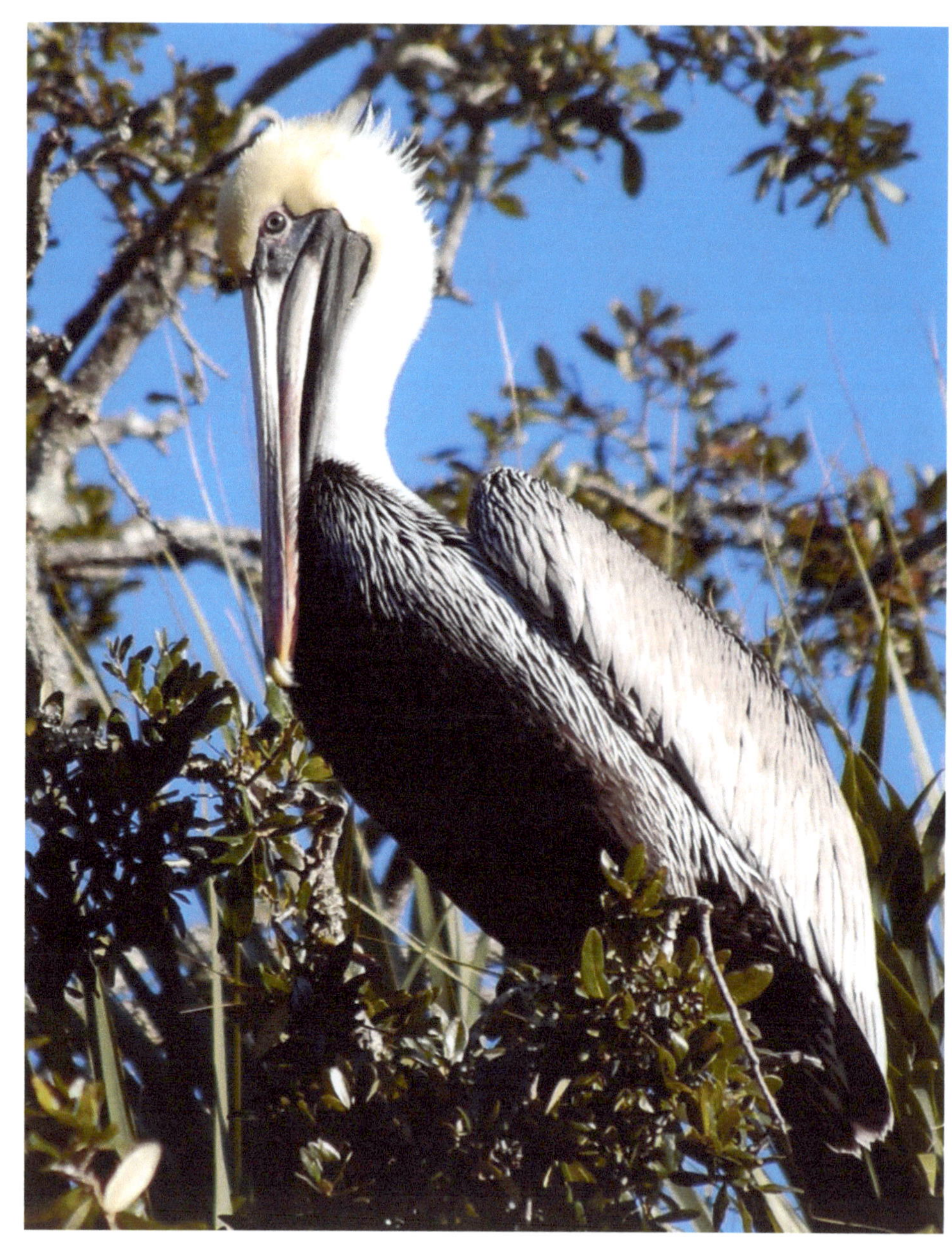

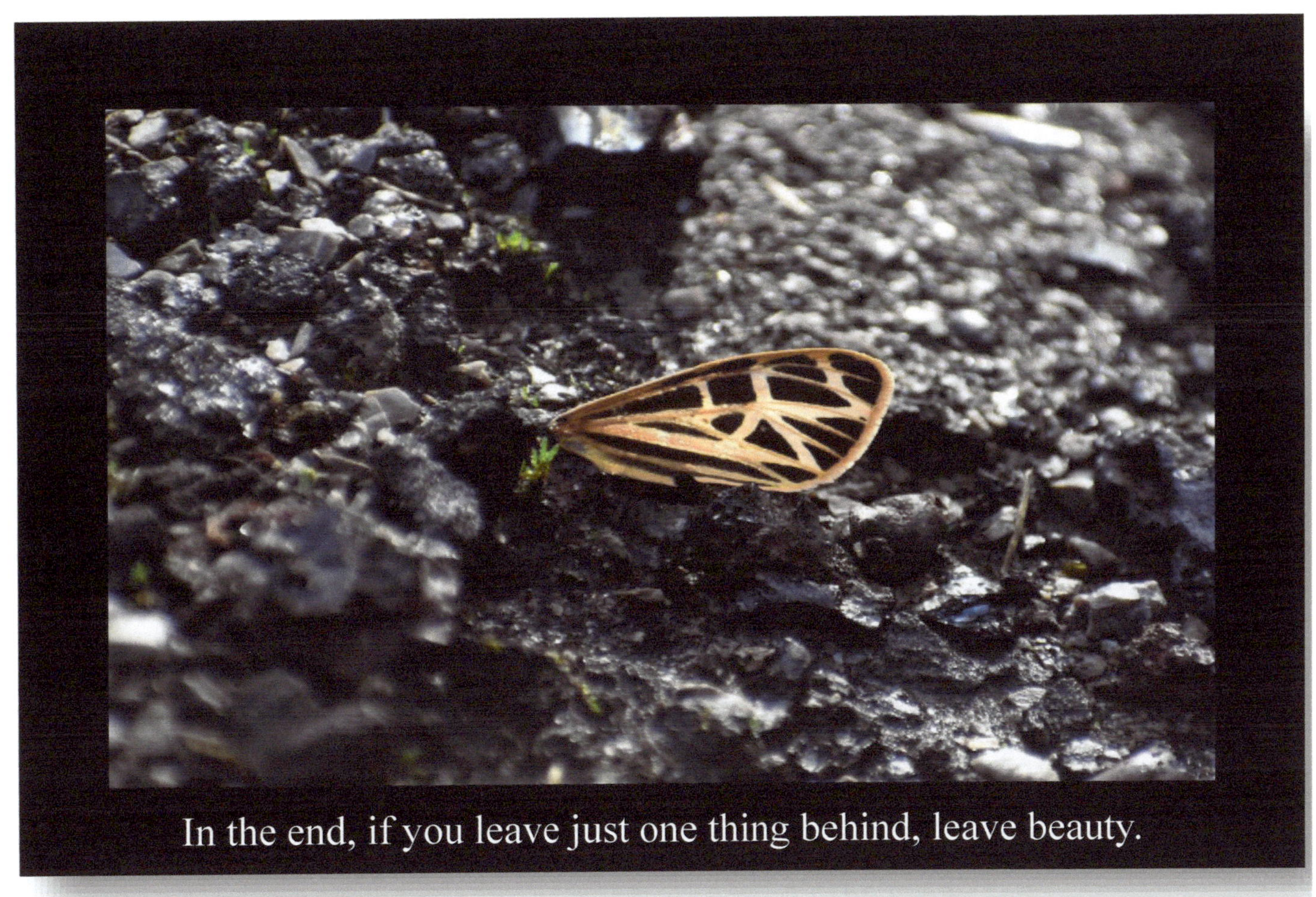

In the end, if you leave just one thing behind, leave beauty.

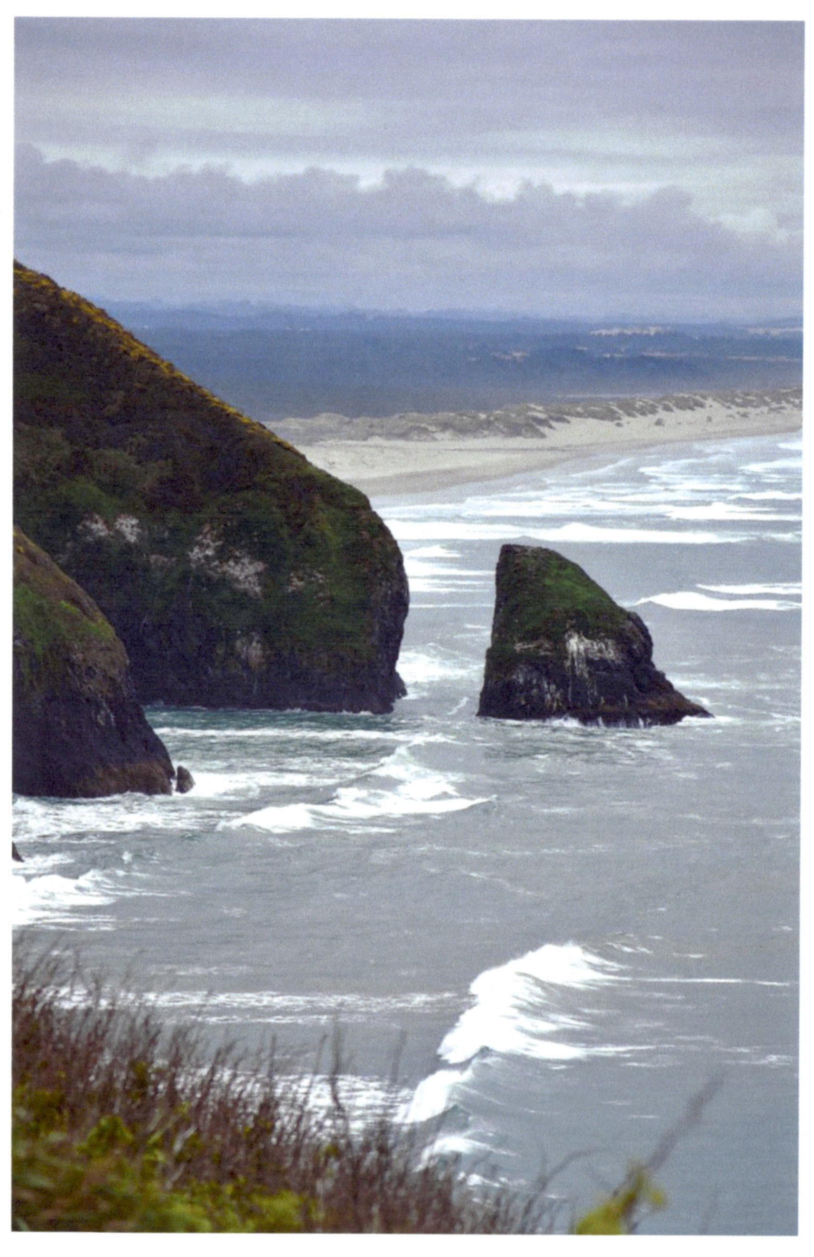

There is nothing like:

A baby's smile

A full moon rising over the ocean

Rubbing a puppy's belly

Autumn in New England

The sound of rain on a tin roof

The sigh of the wind in a forest

Your first love, your last love

Sitting alone in a silent church

Singing loudly and being silly with your friends

Standing on top of your first mountain

Watching the sun sink into the sea

Giggles

Holding the hand of your grandma

Making your first cake

Standing in a wind storm on a beach

Sitting in the driver's seat of your first car

Getting your first "real" paycheck

Making snow angels

Just like our cars and
furnaces, our own filters
need to be changed
occasionally.

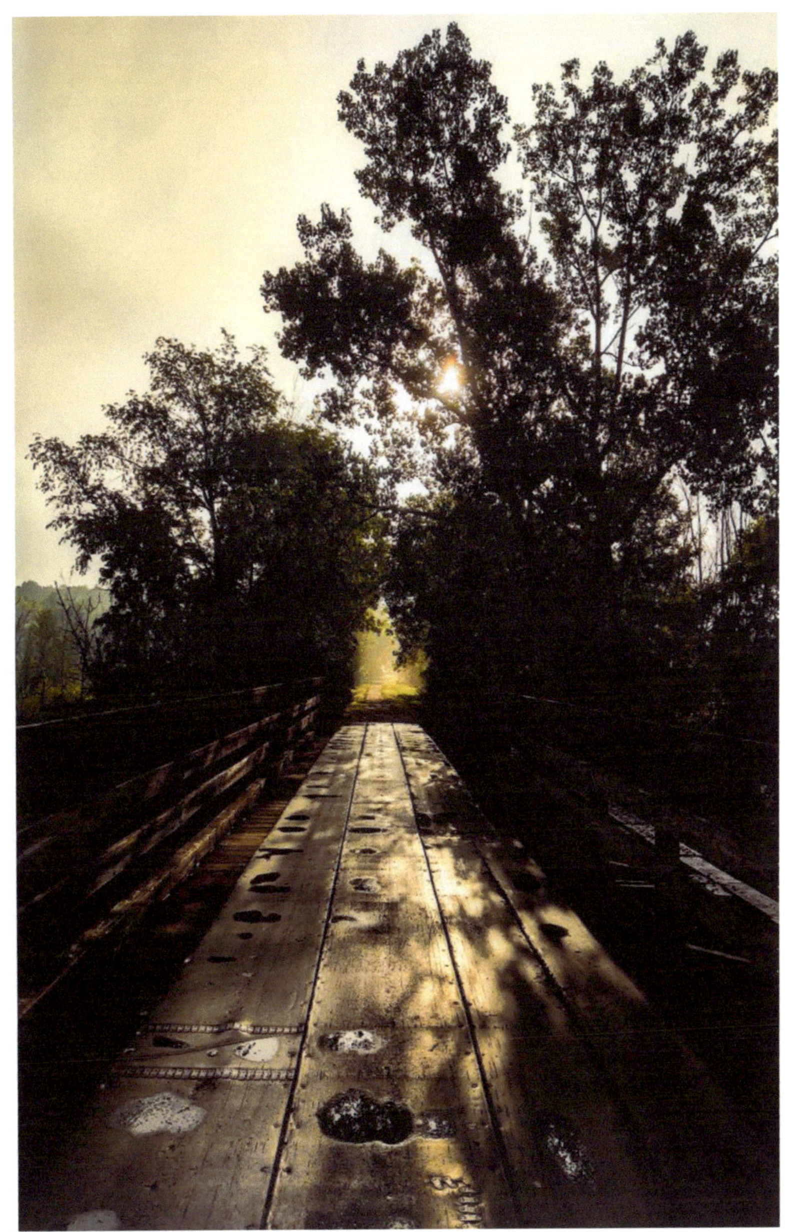

Instinctual fear is the
only kind you should
really listen to and
act on.

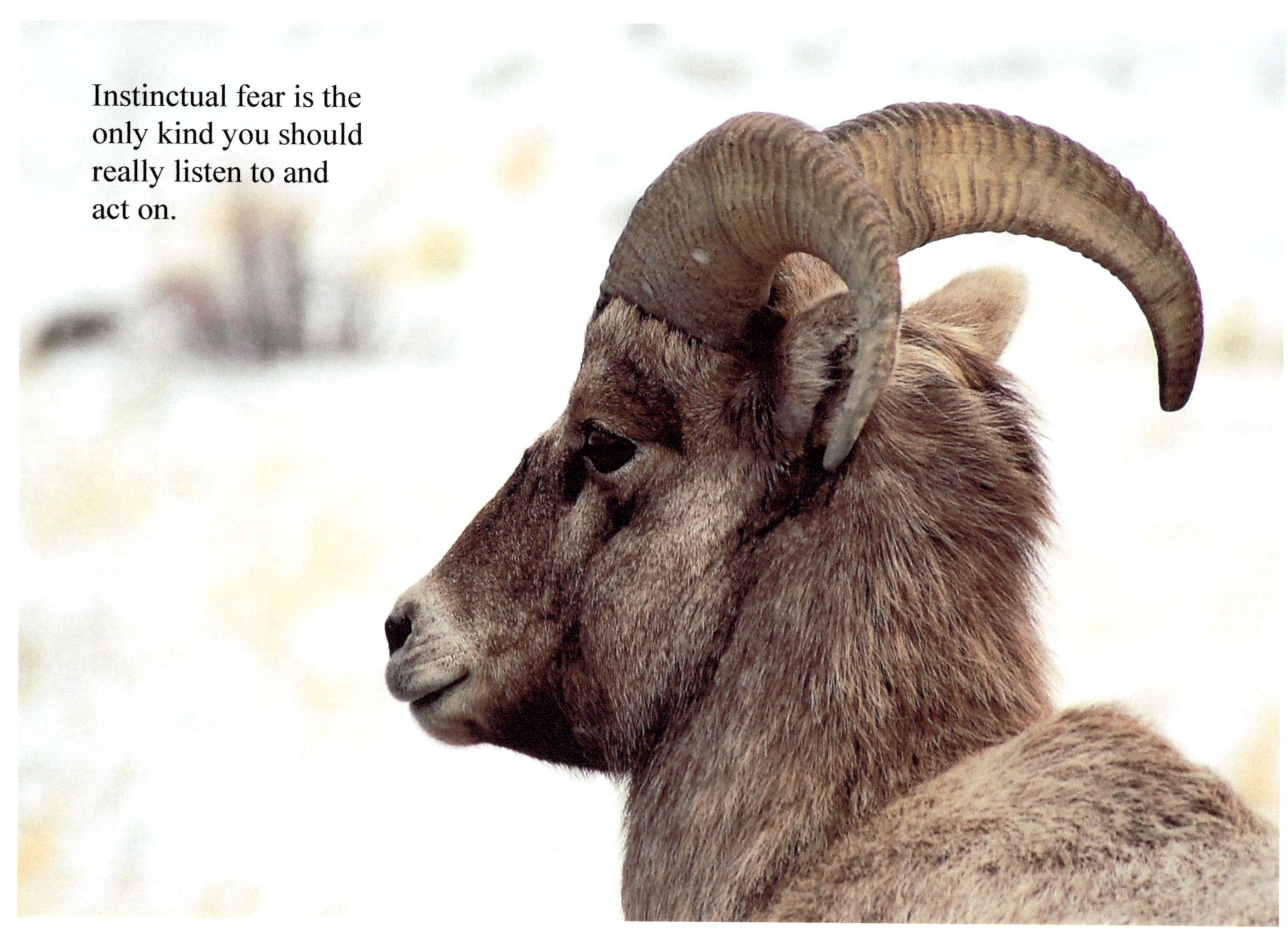

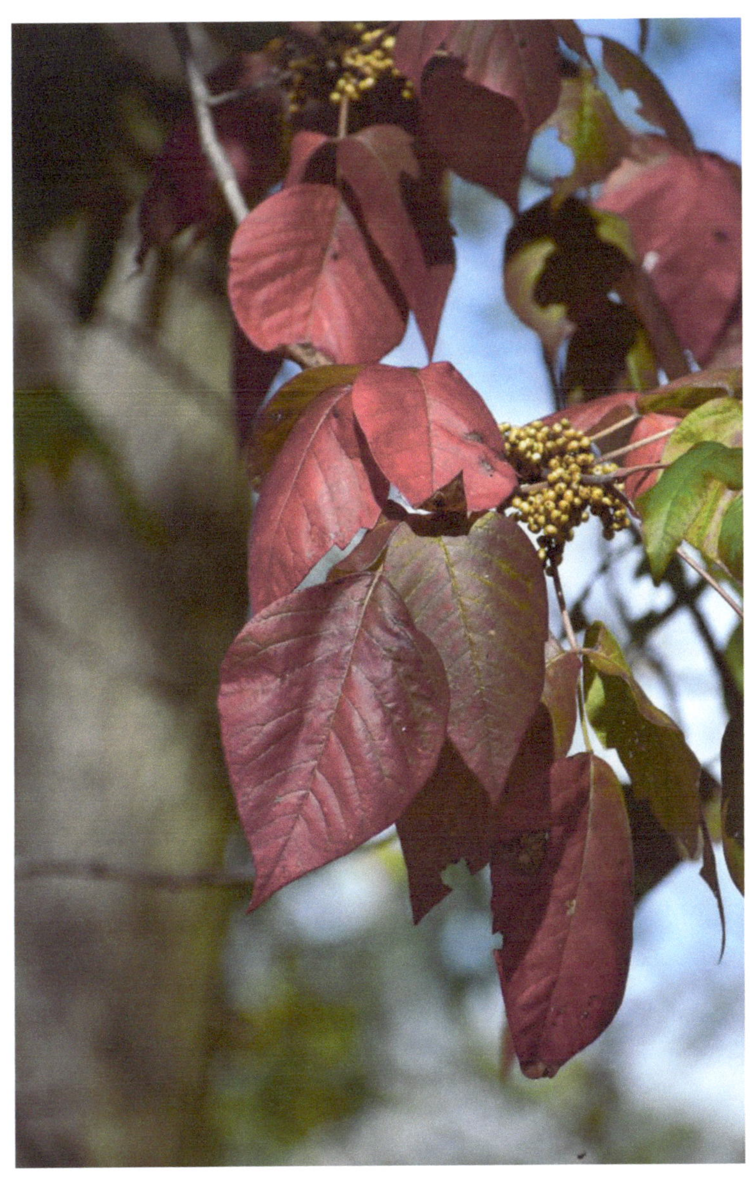

I have a theory: when you
share your doughnut with
someone; even if it's just
a bite, all the calories go
with that bite. It's God's
way of rewarding you for
sharing. It's my theory
and I'm sticking to it.

The best advice I could give to young women is to go "find" themselves. Figuratively, look under your bed and in your closets. Find all your strengths and weaknesses. Go back to your childhood reflect on all the good and the bad … learn to forgive those who acted badly towards you. Realize that you are you based on these interactions, but that they don't have to define you. Work until you can forgive them their mistakes and their flaws. They are human, after all.

Learn to forgive yourself for the mistakes you've made, especially if you learned the lesson that came from them. Be okay with your lack of perfection—let's face it, you're not perfect nor should you want to be. Wrap your arms around what makes you ... you! Love yourself for all of your bugaboos. Once you understand what makes you tick you will be better able to handle anything that comes your way. Strength comes from knowing who you are. You are you first!

Knowing this before you become someone's spouse, or someone's mother is the healing that will help you move forward and allow you to develop your core strength. Believe me, it's easier to do this when you are young than in mid-life, and almost impossible at age eighty.

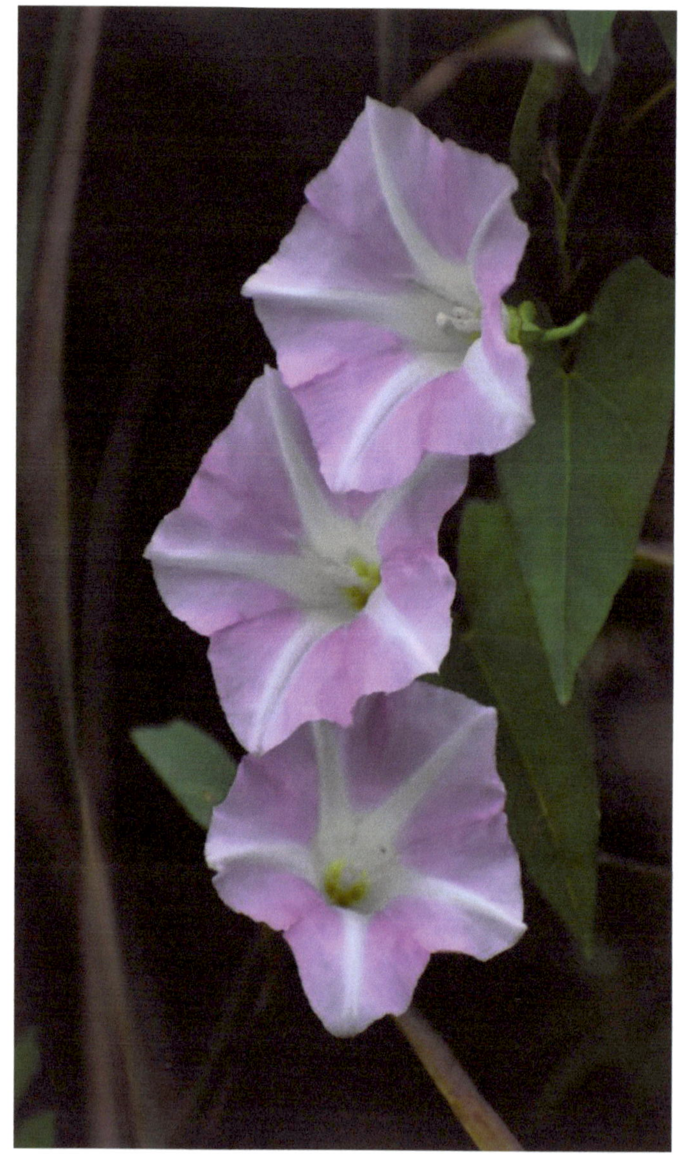

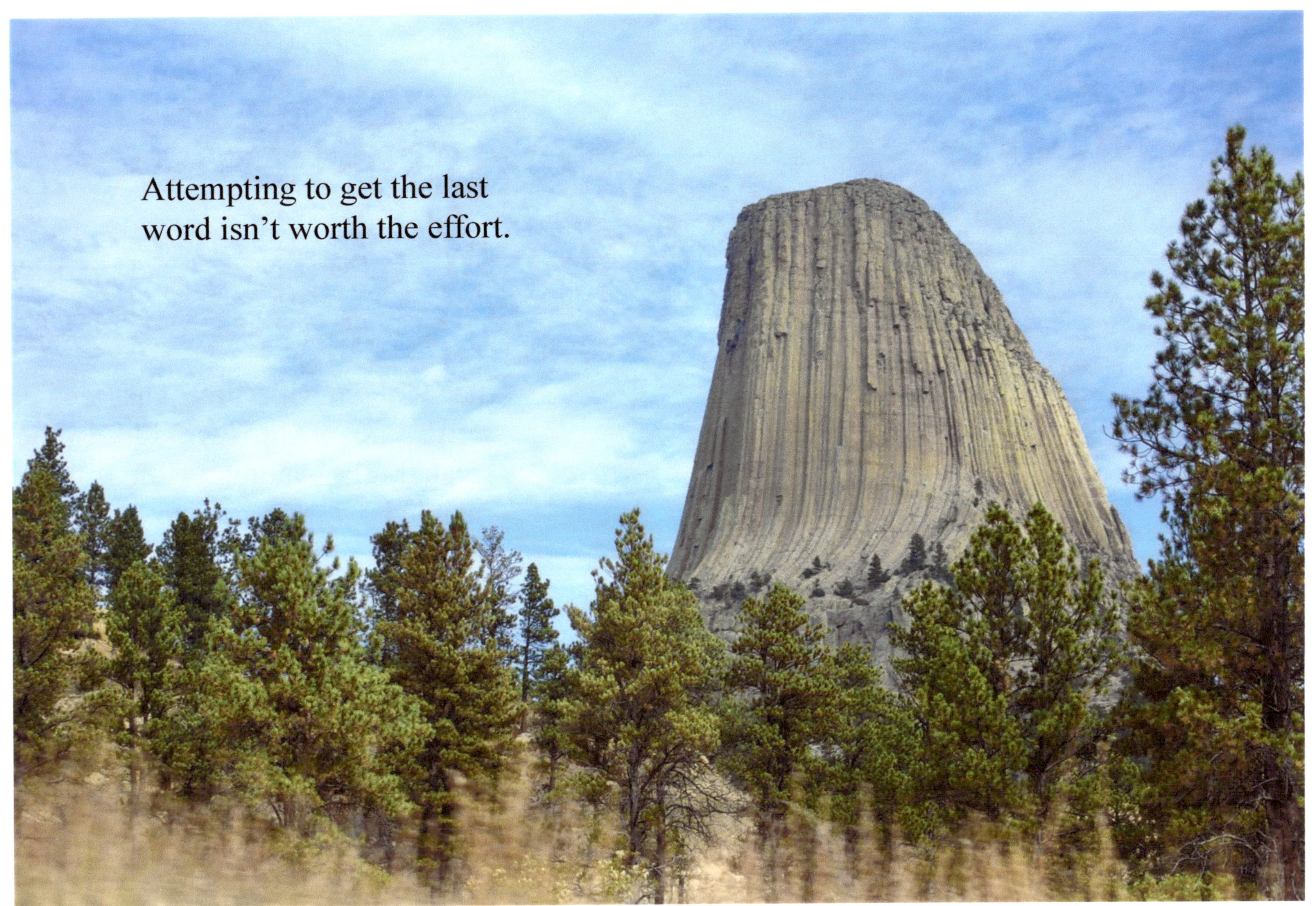
Attempting to get the last
word isn't worth the effort.

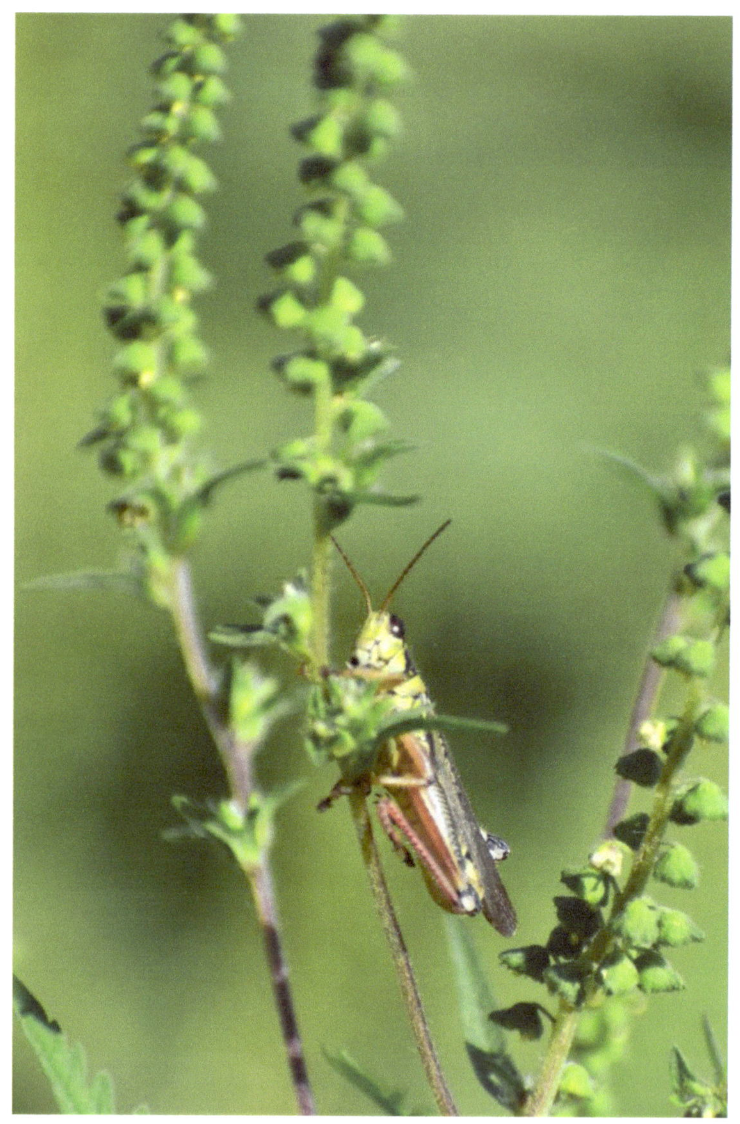

The Golden Rule states that we need to treat people how we'd like to be treated. The Platinum Rule is to treat people how they want to be treated. There is a difference.

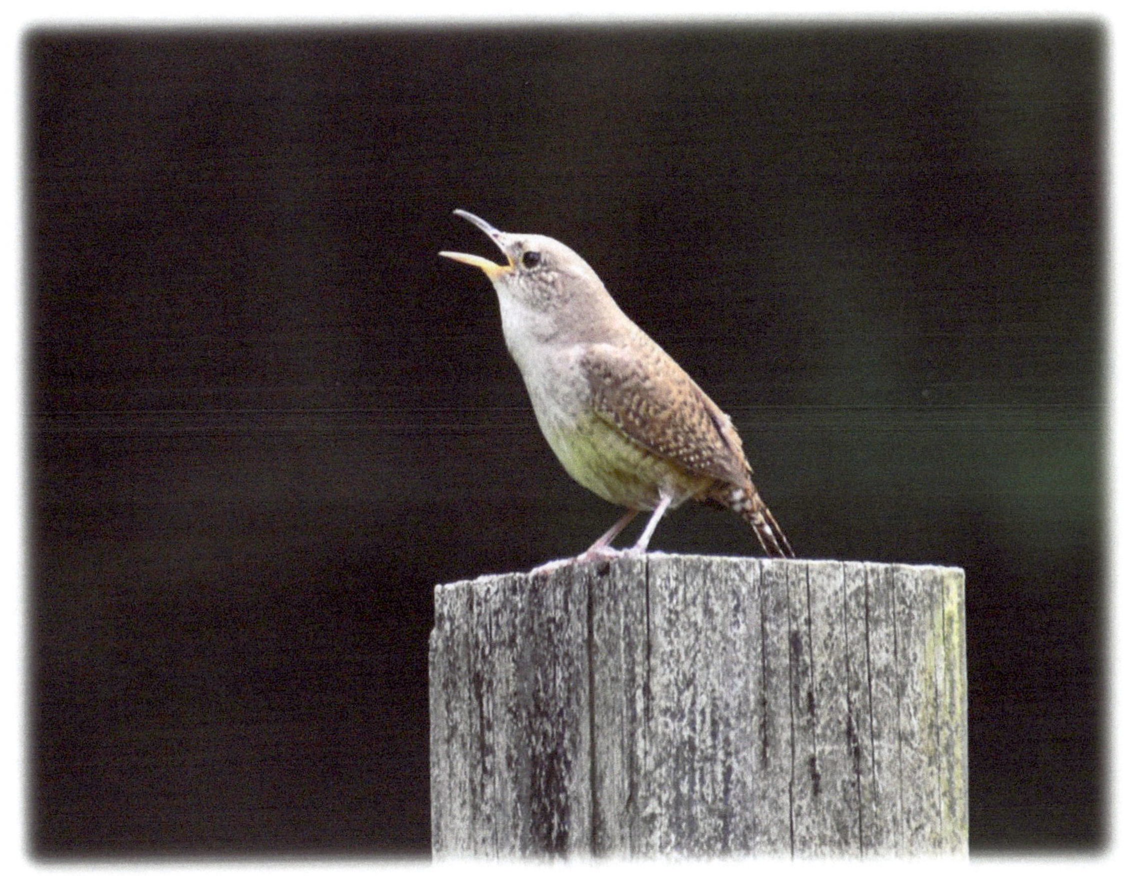

They say that the apple doesn't fall to far from the tree.
That could be considered a compliment or an insult.
It depends on the tree.

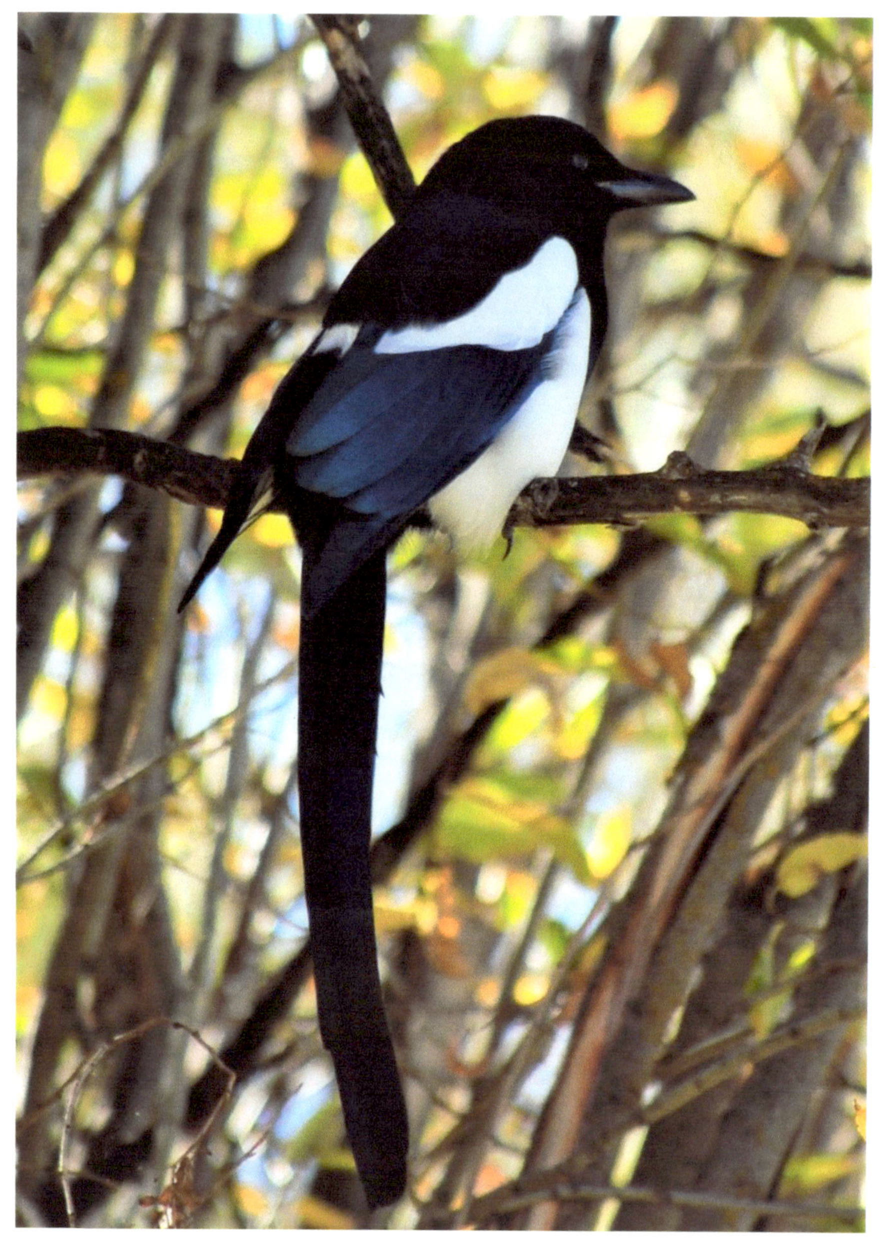

In your life I wish more of the word "and" and less of the word "or".

I hope you never live to regret the saying: one of these days.

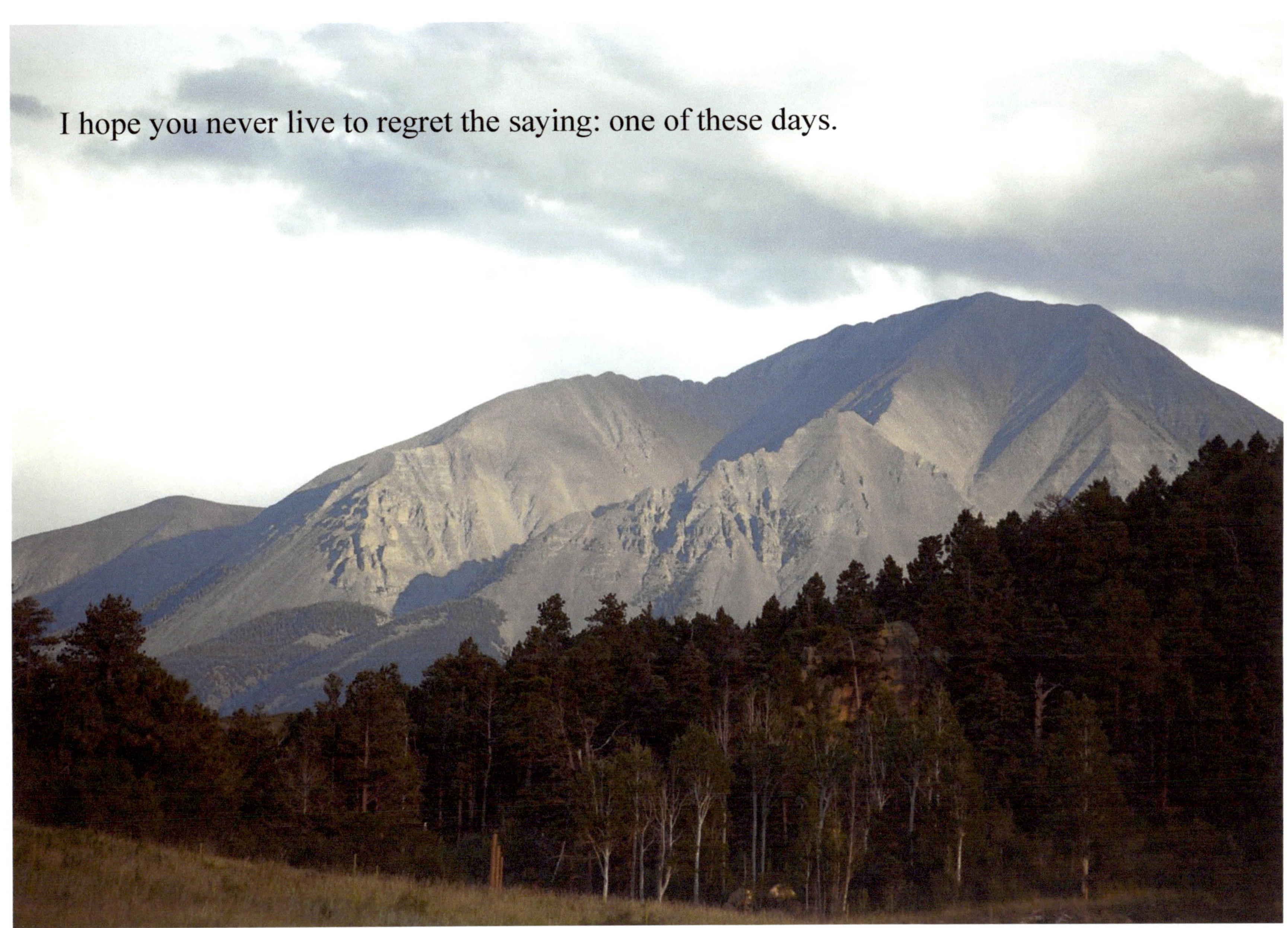

It's important to know the difference between:

Being kind

Being generous

Being forgiving

And being stupid

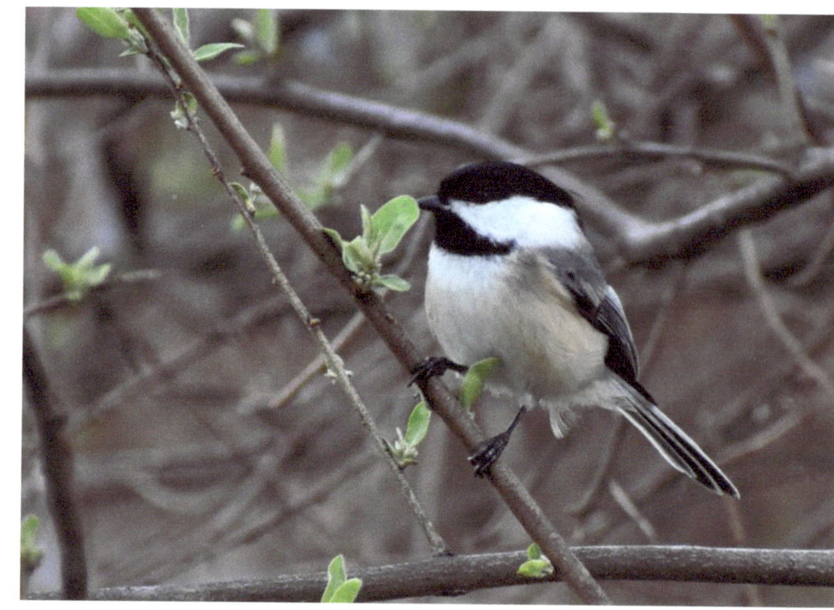

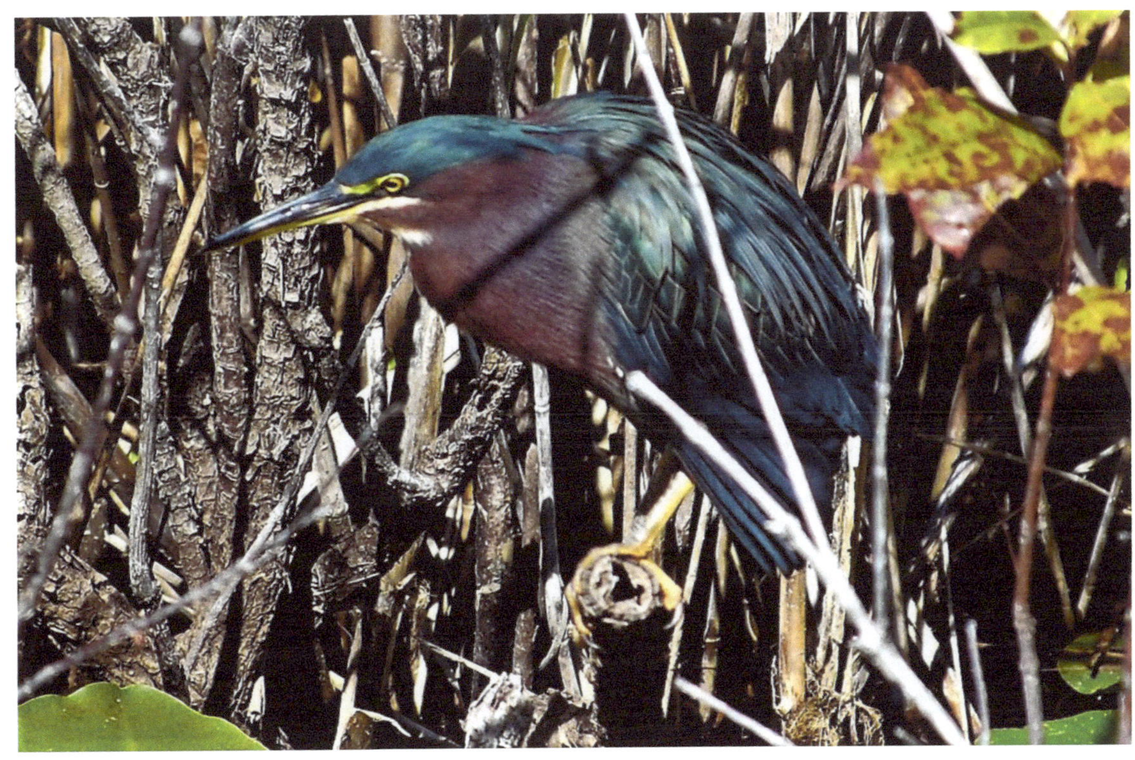

Don't let anyone paint over your true colors.

Faith gets you through the fear of the unknown.

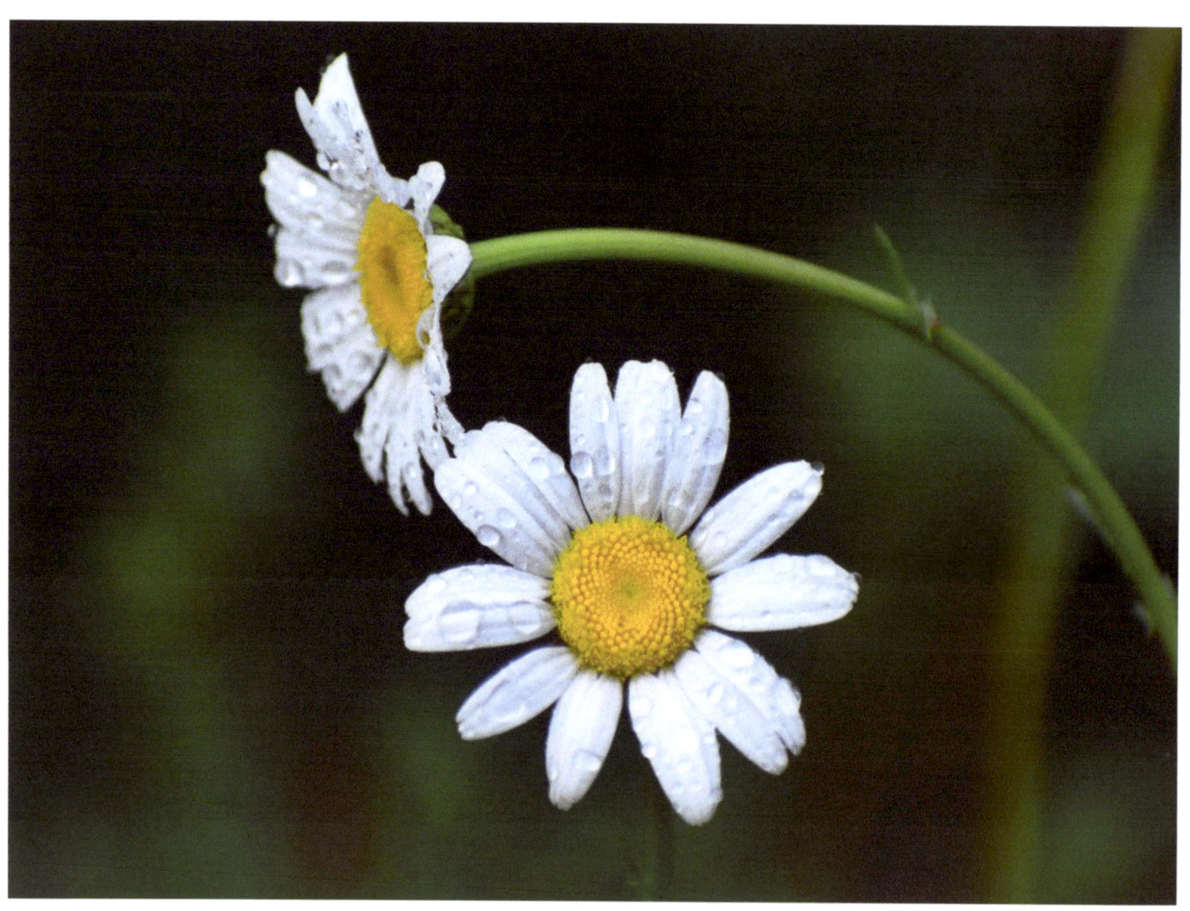

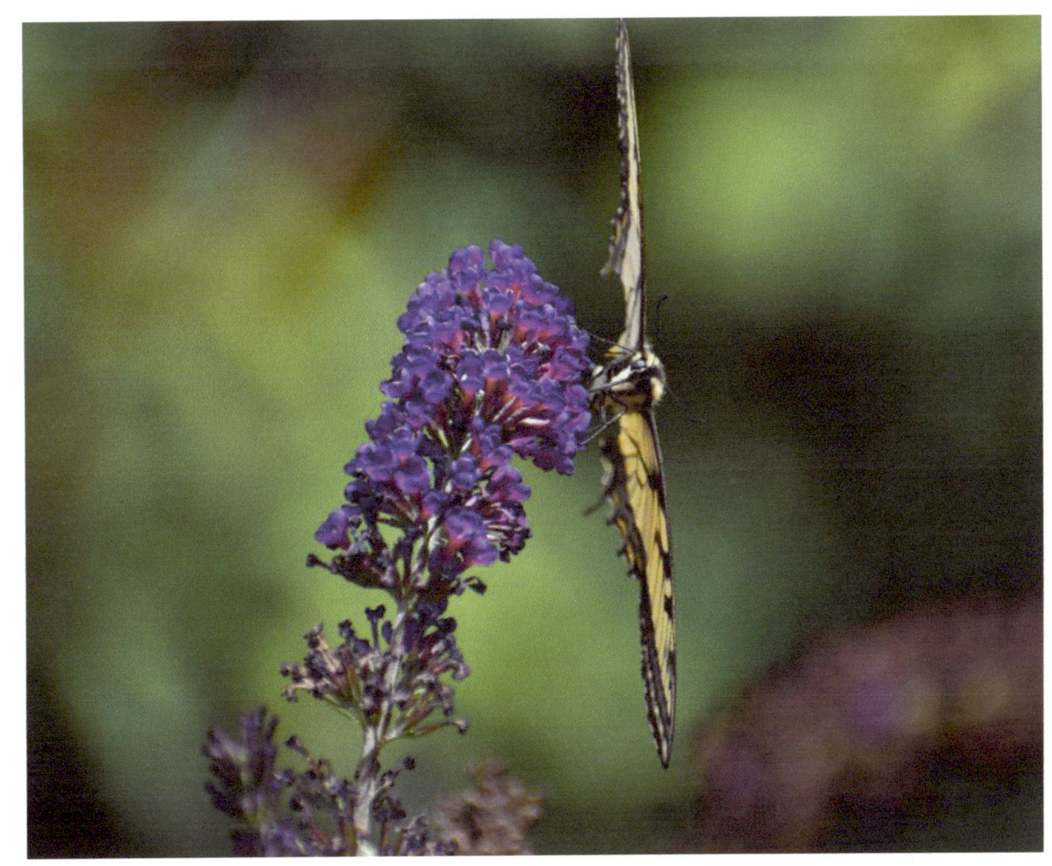

Admit when you are wrong, humbly.

Our opinions aren't wrong, because
they are based on our perceptions.
How we defend our opinions could
probably use some work.

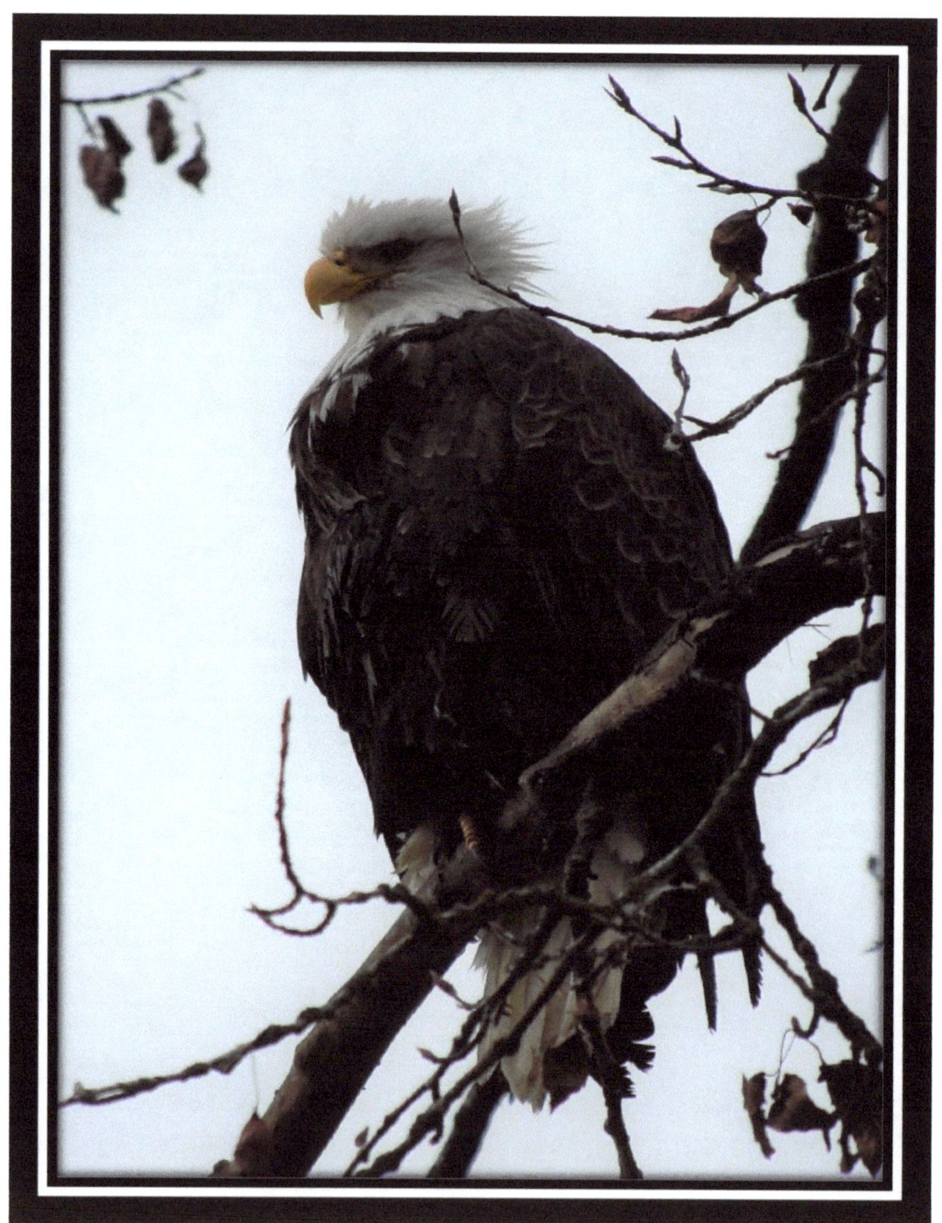

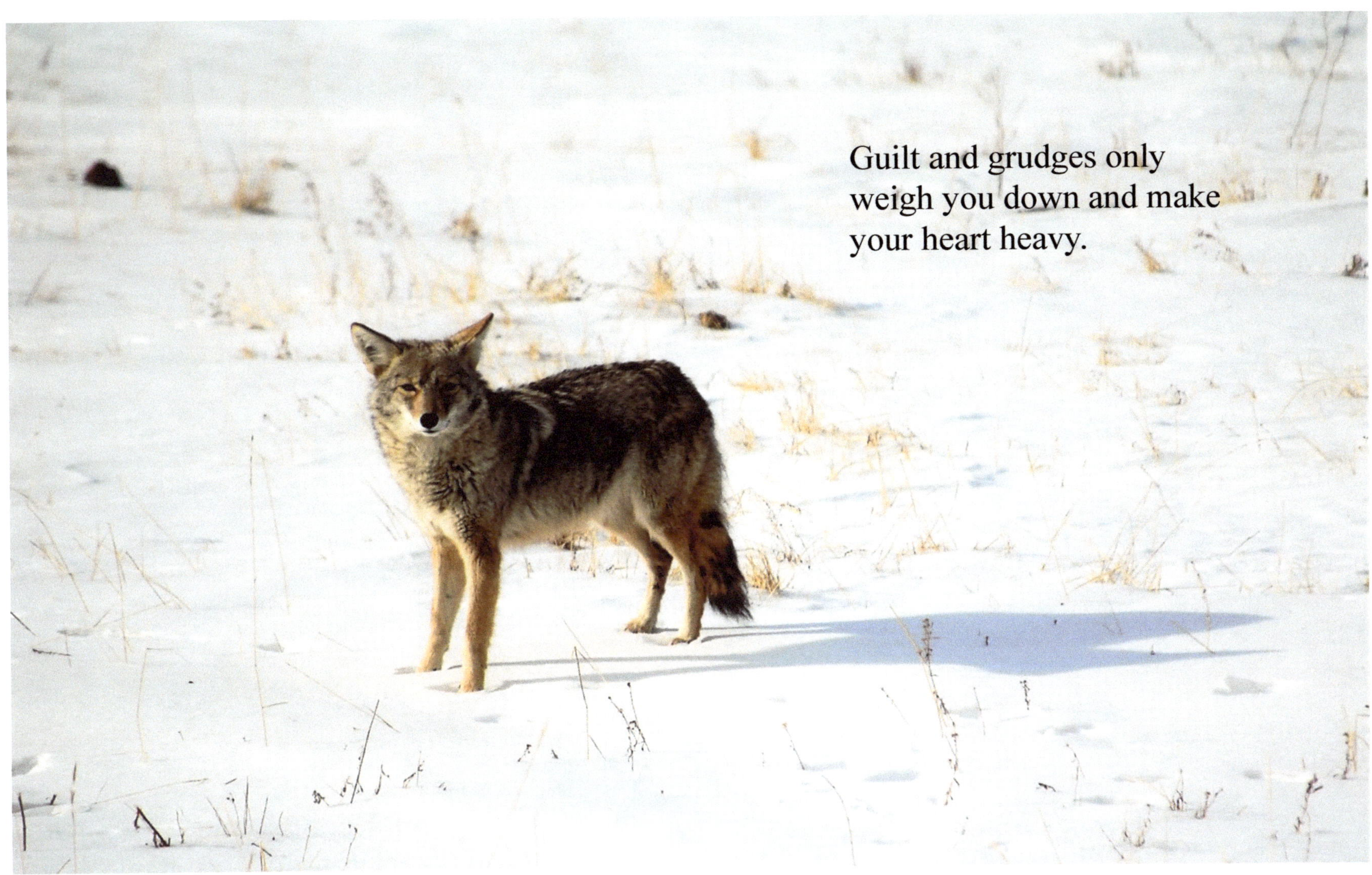
Guilt and grudges only
weigh you down and make
your heart heavy.

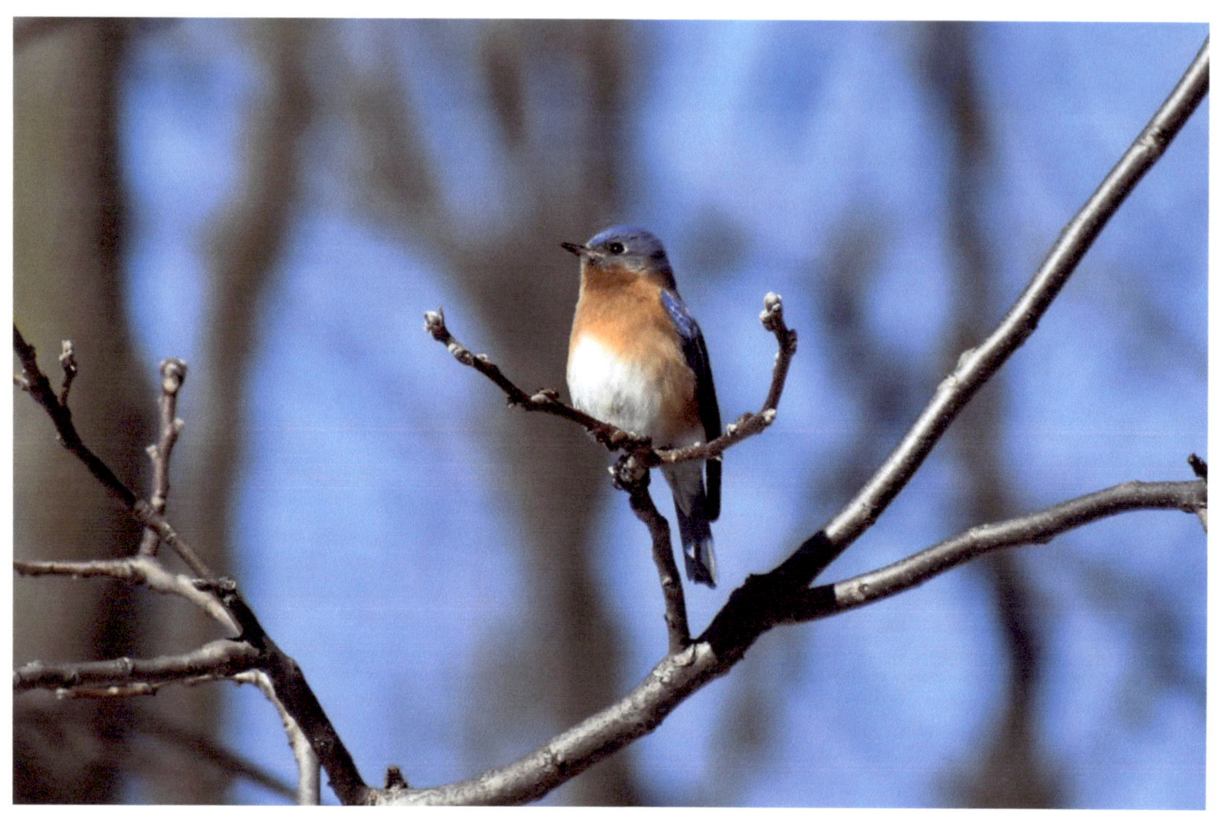

It is unreasonable to try and reason with
someone who is unreasonable.

Save the planet, one "something" at a time.

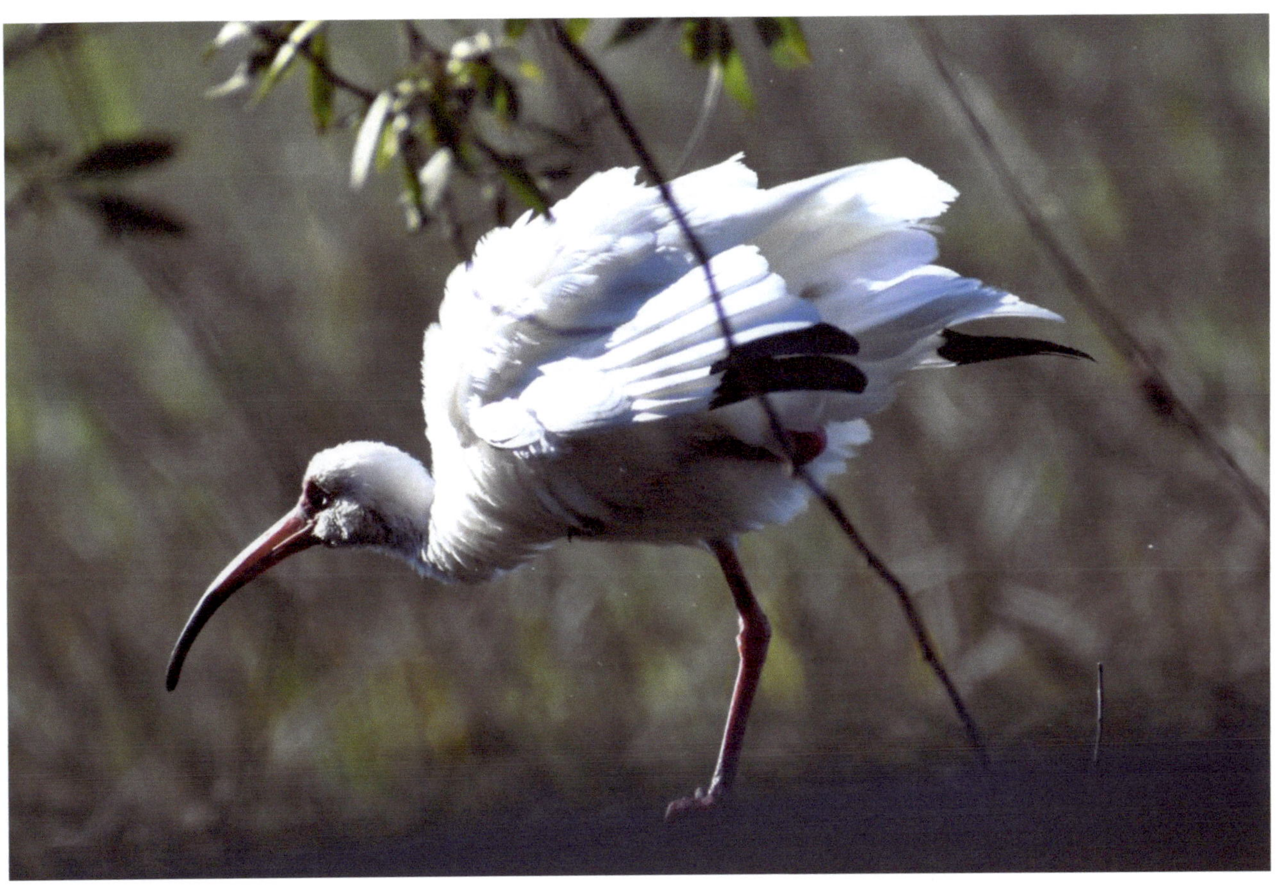

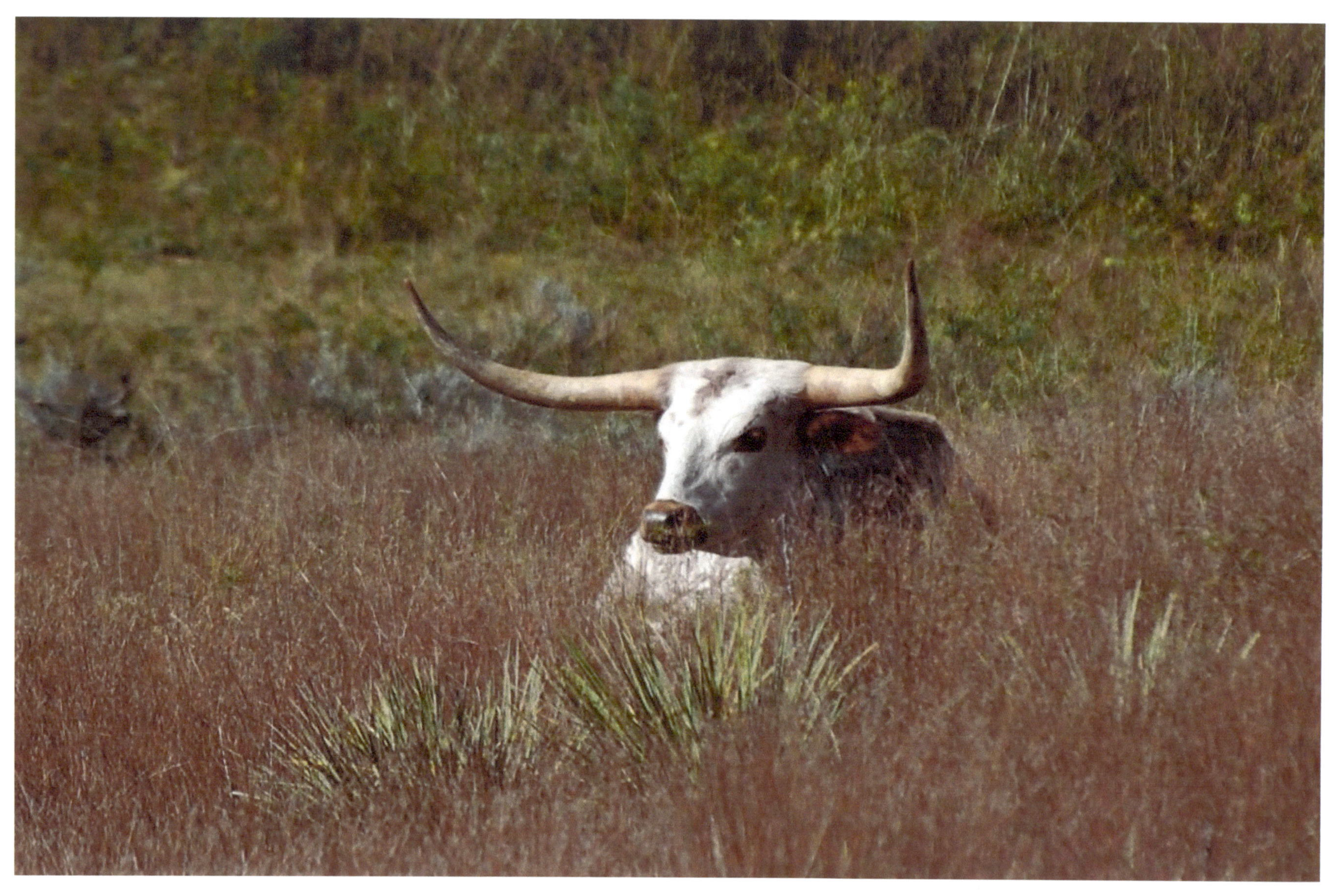

A bull in a china shop will only accomplish one thing: broken dishes.

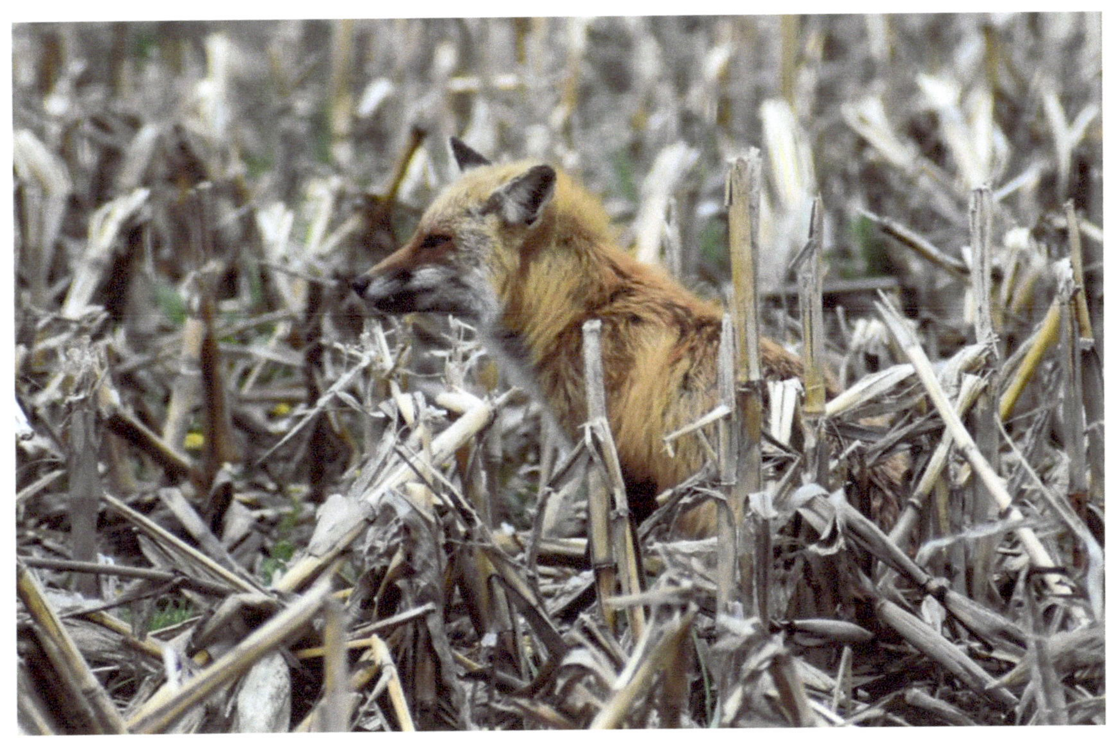

When listening to someone, the only agenda you should have is to learn something.

There is never any more than a 100
percent effort. If you give your all,
that's all you have.

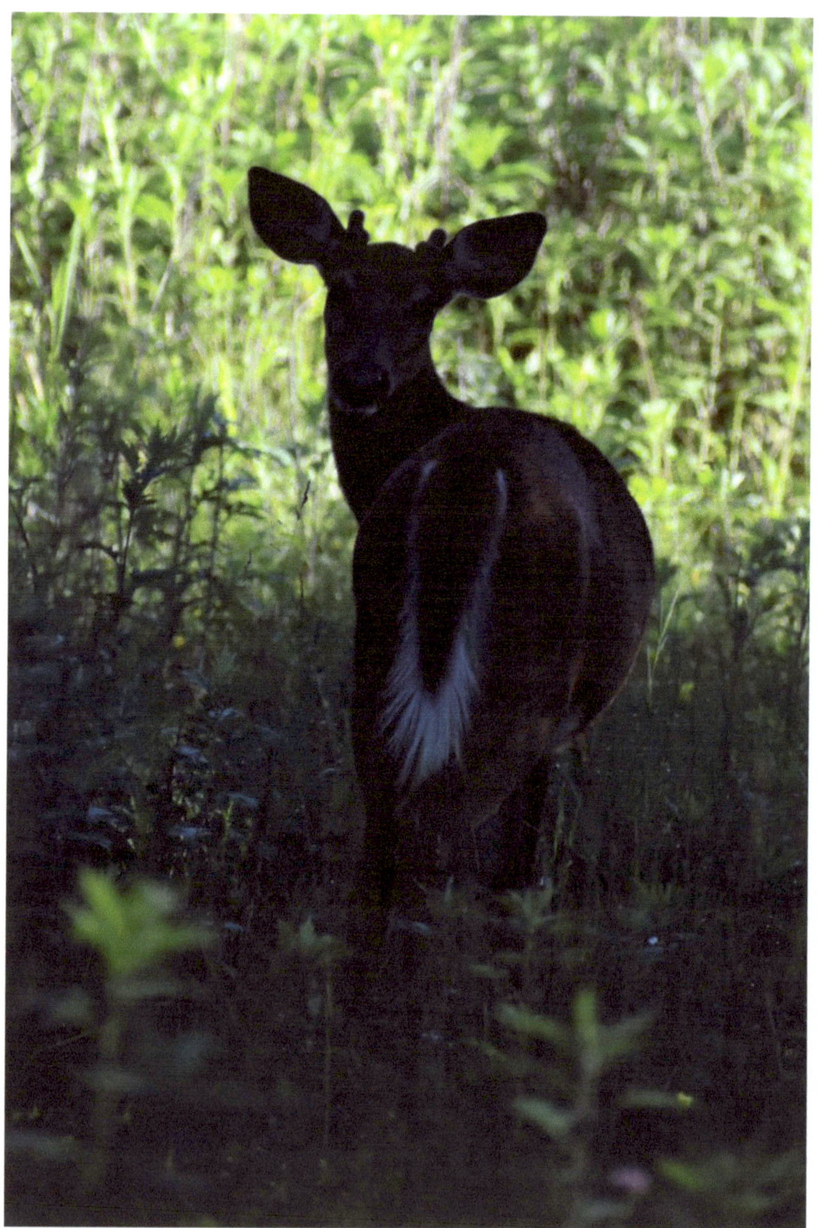

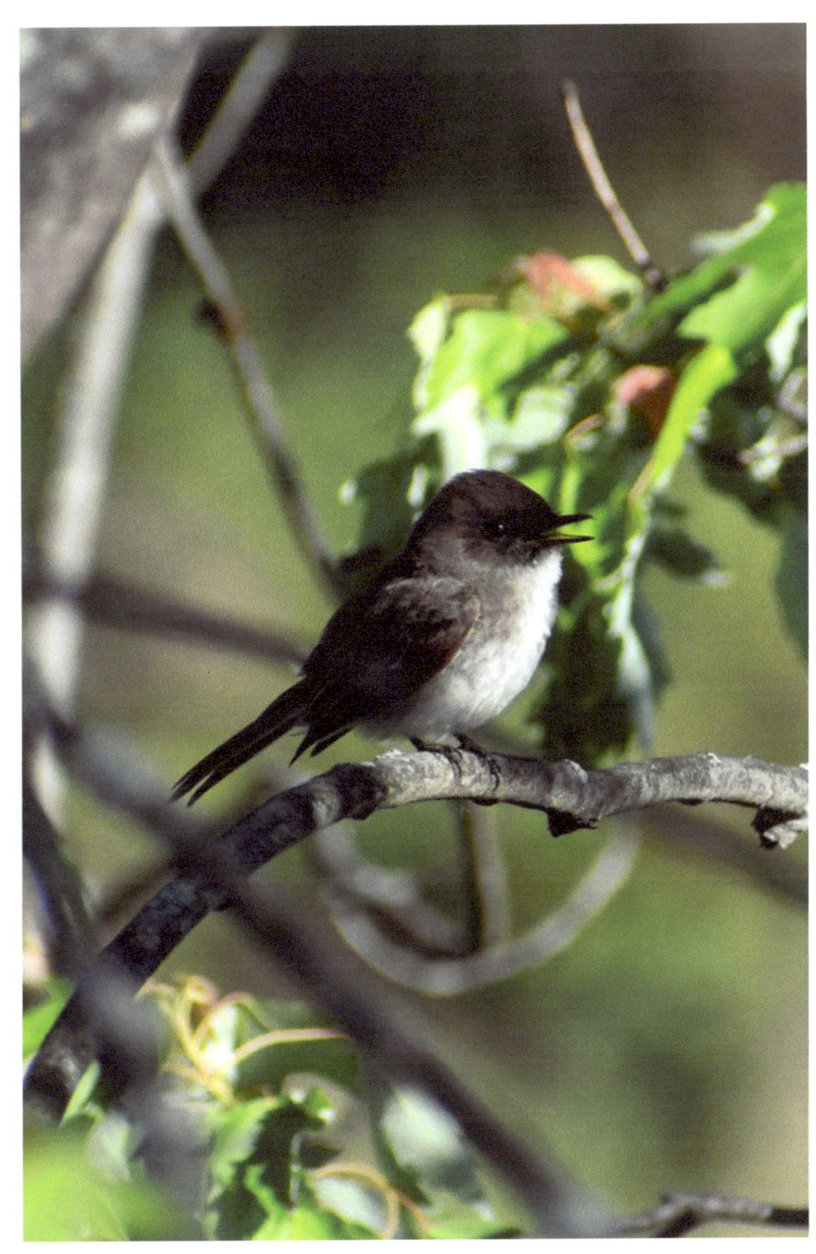

There are things and people in your life that:

You should quit.

You can't quit.

You will never quit.

It's important to know the difference.

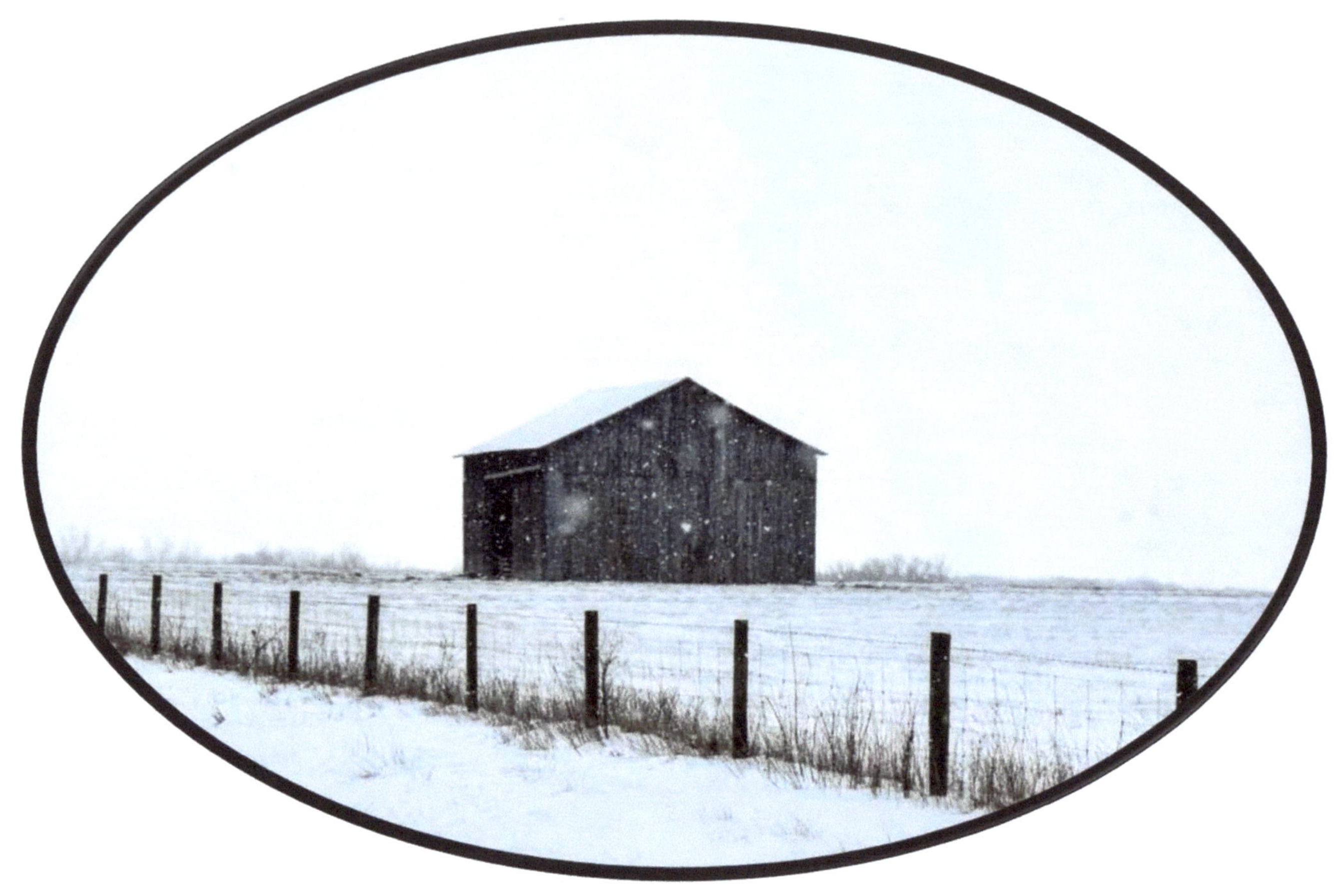

Happiness is achieved once you stop worrying what other people think of you.

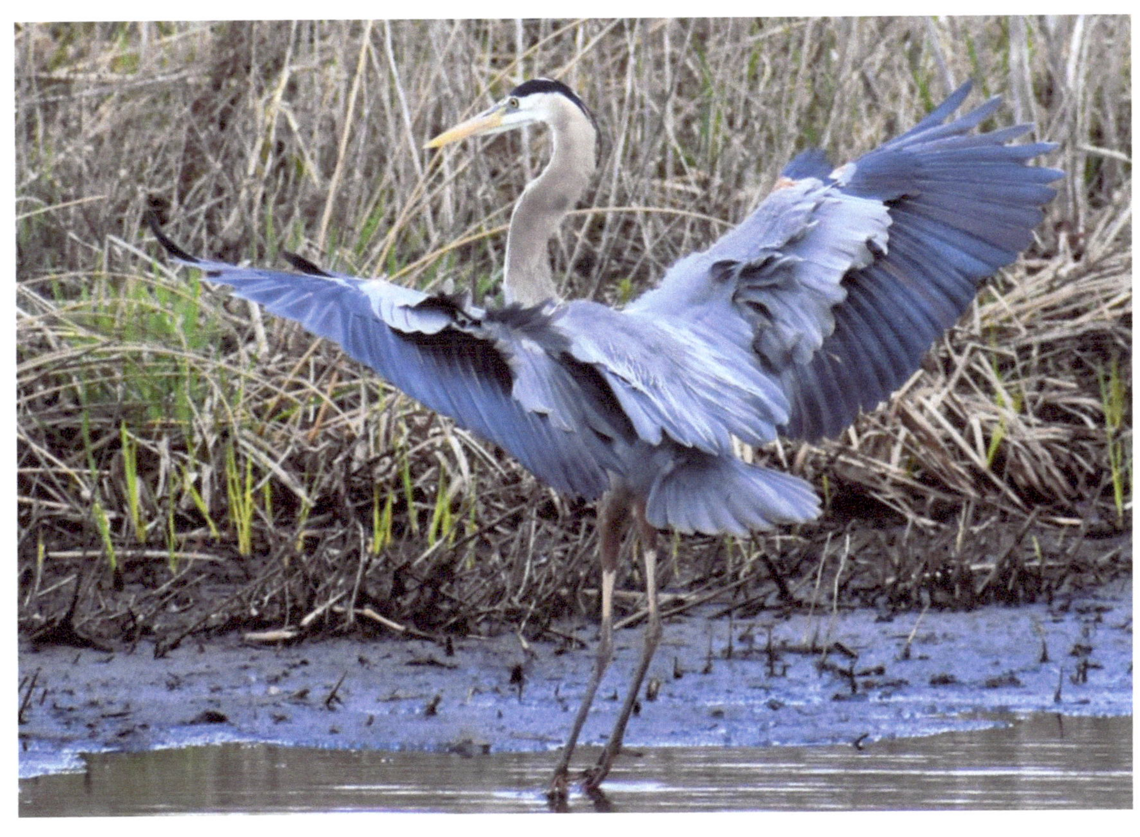

Inspiration comes from being inspired by another.
Who have you inspired today?

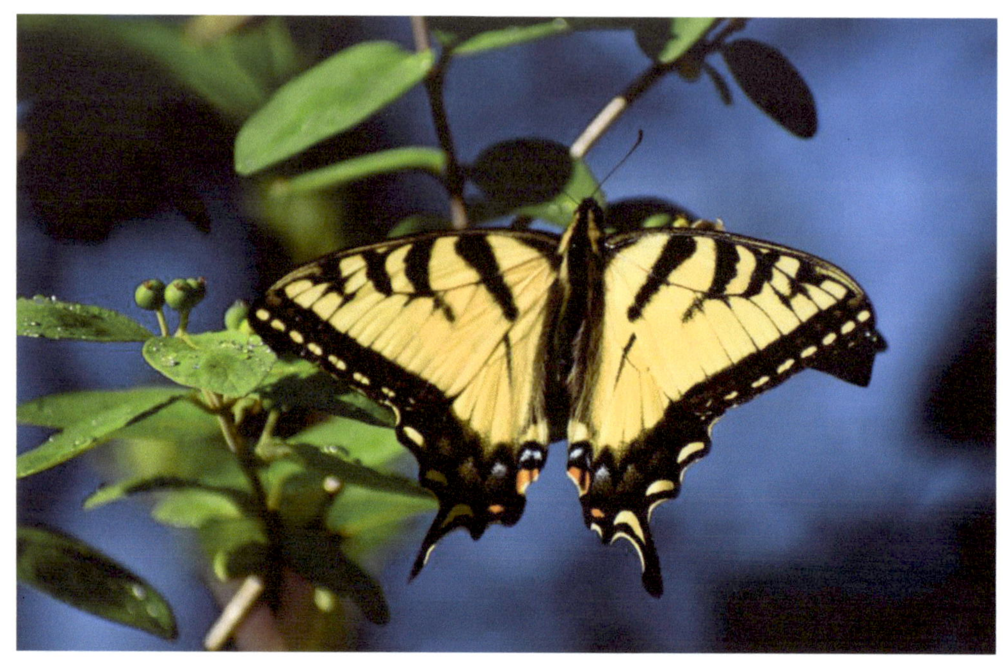

Summon strength from inside.

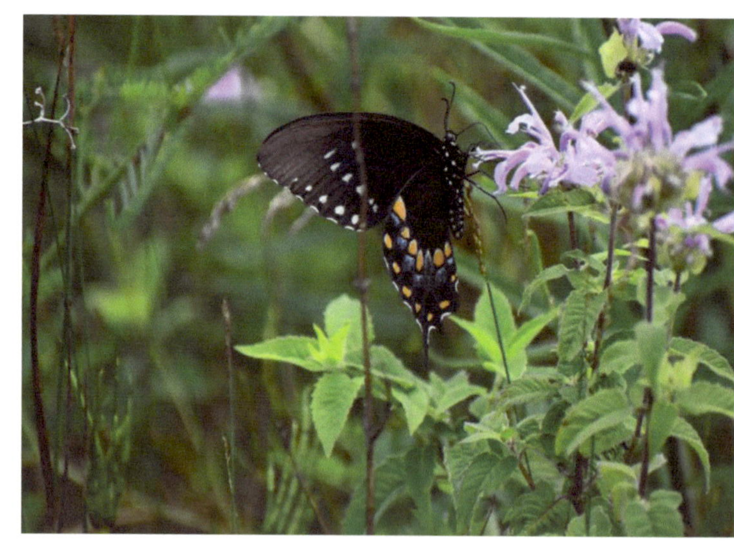

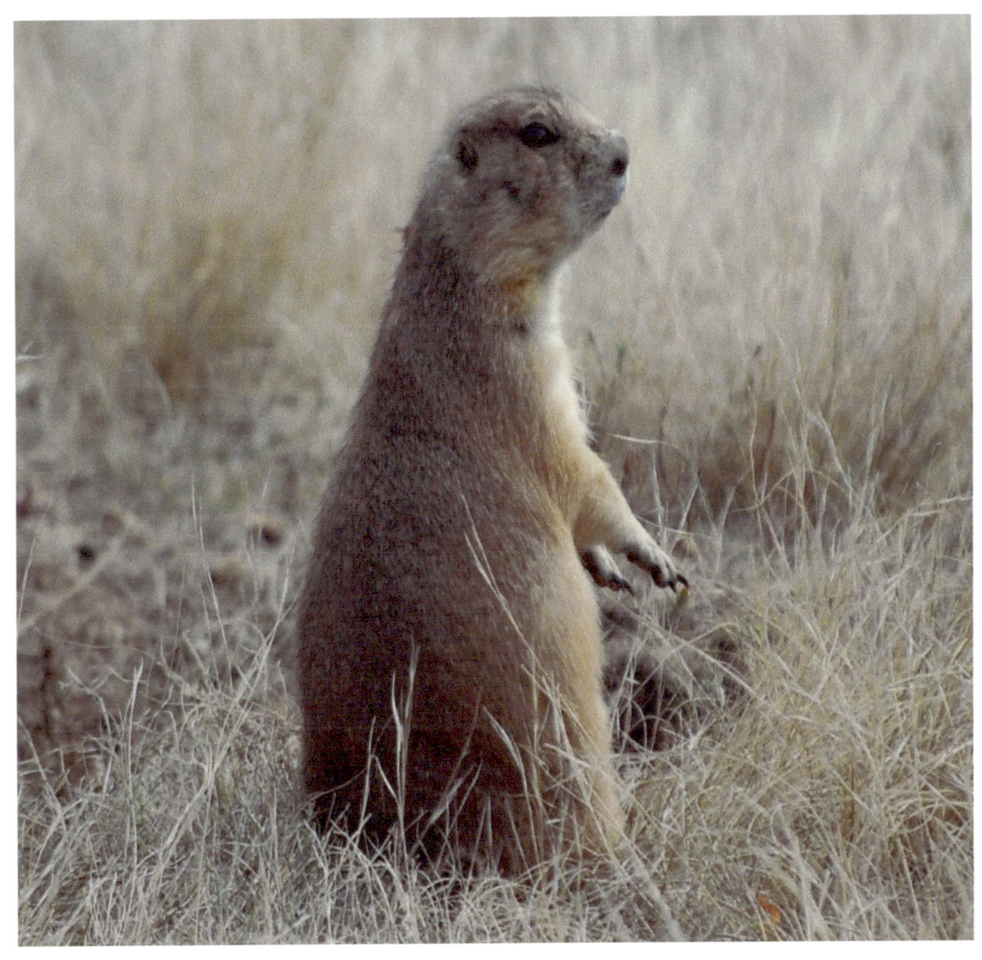

Every now and again you will get kicked in the teeth. When that happens, smile. Even if you land up toothless, keep smiling.

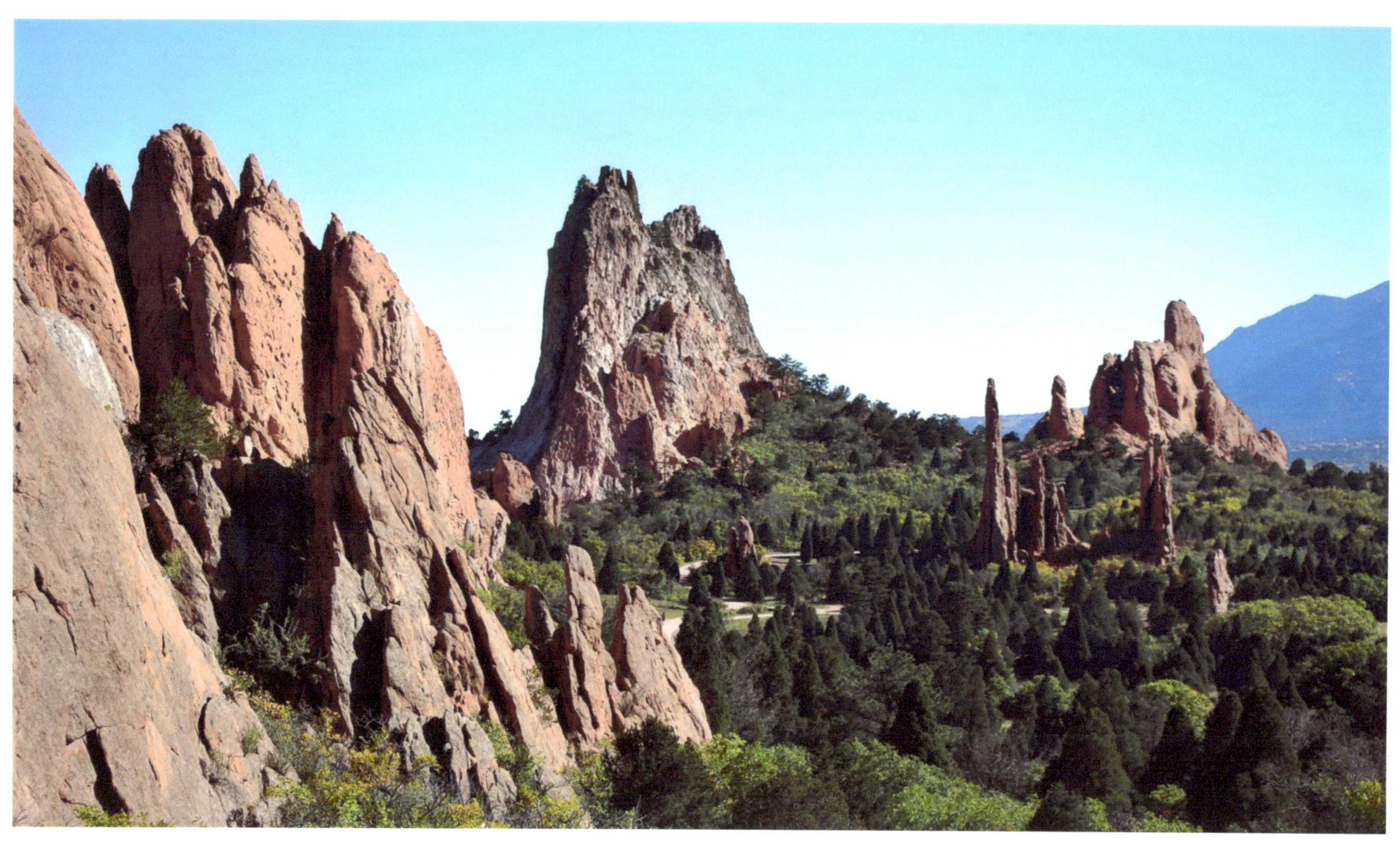

You should be honest. You just don't have to be brutal about it.

Taking responsibility for your actions
means to remove any "what about"
and "no, but…."

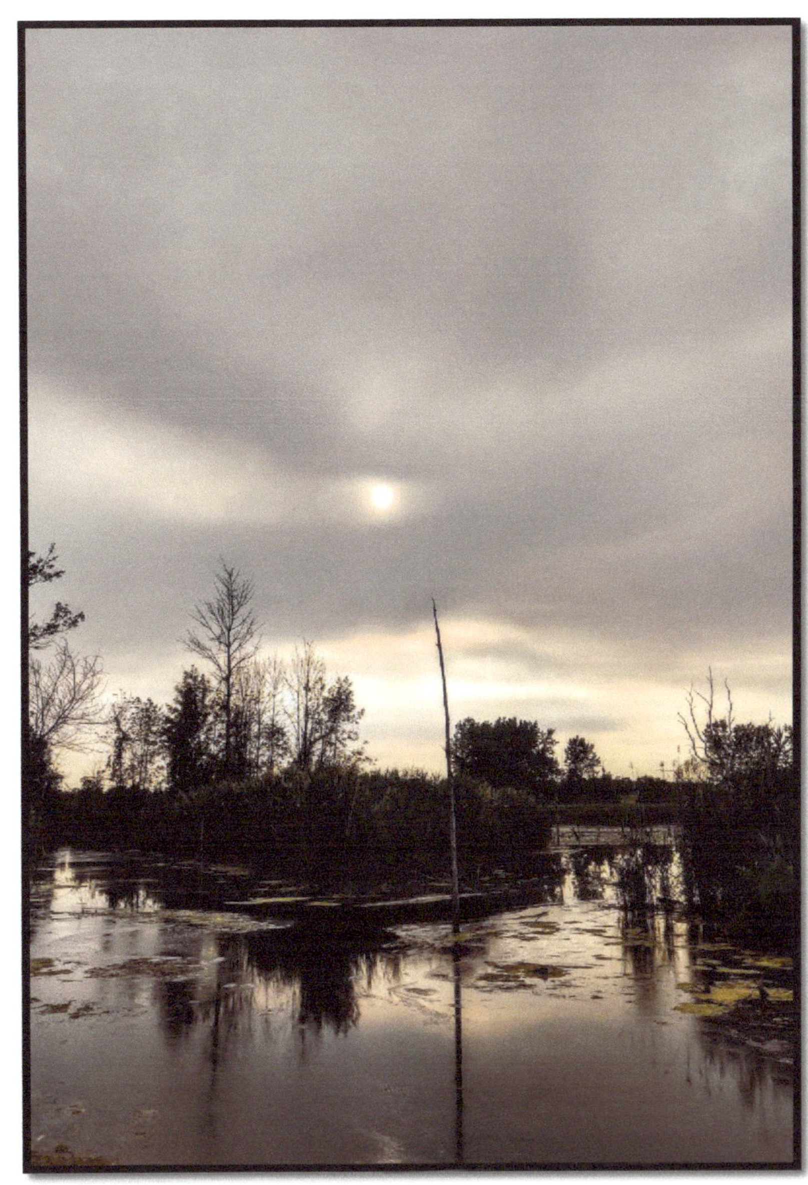

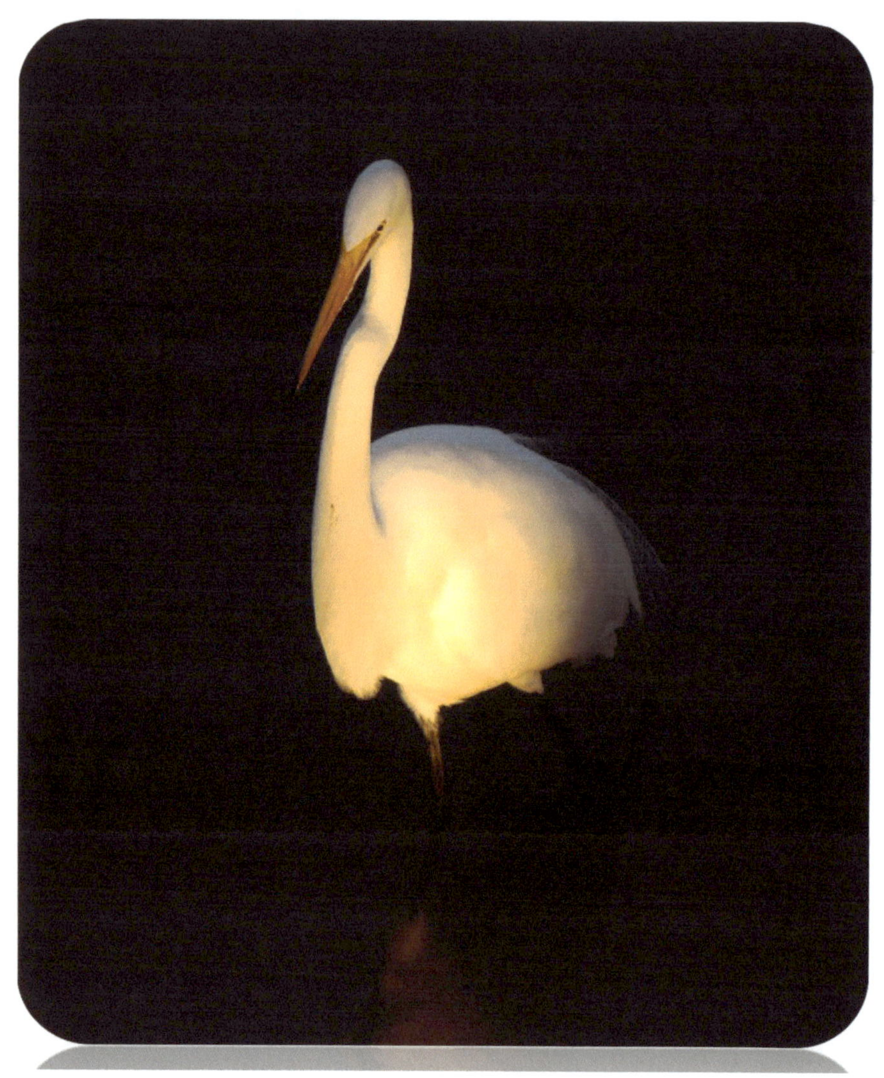

Humans: the only species on the
planet that intentionally destroy their
own habitat.

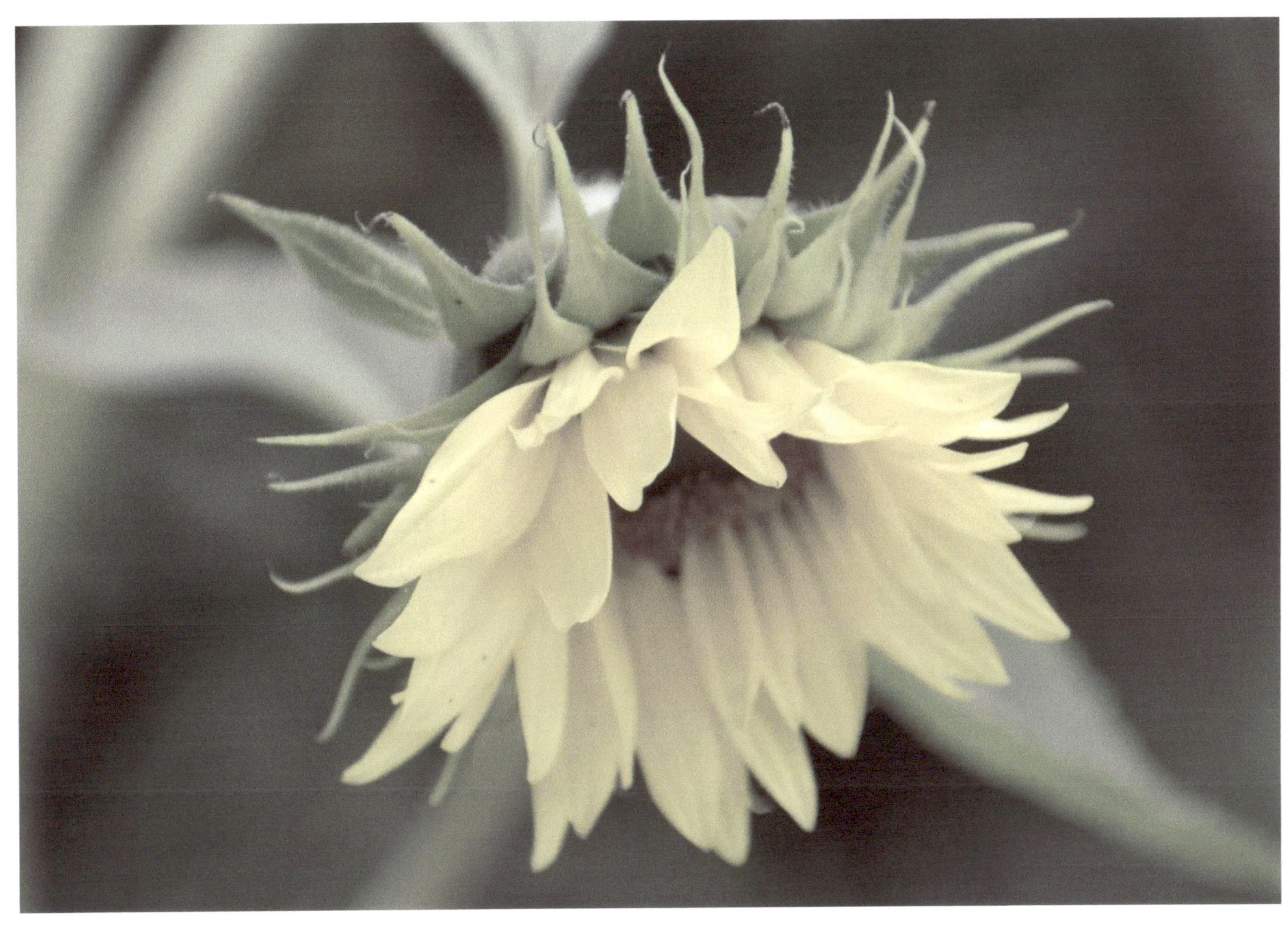

There are times in our lives when we feel like we have hit rock bottom.
This is when God finally gets your attention.

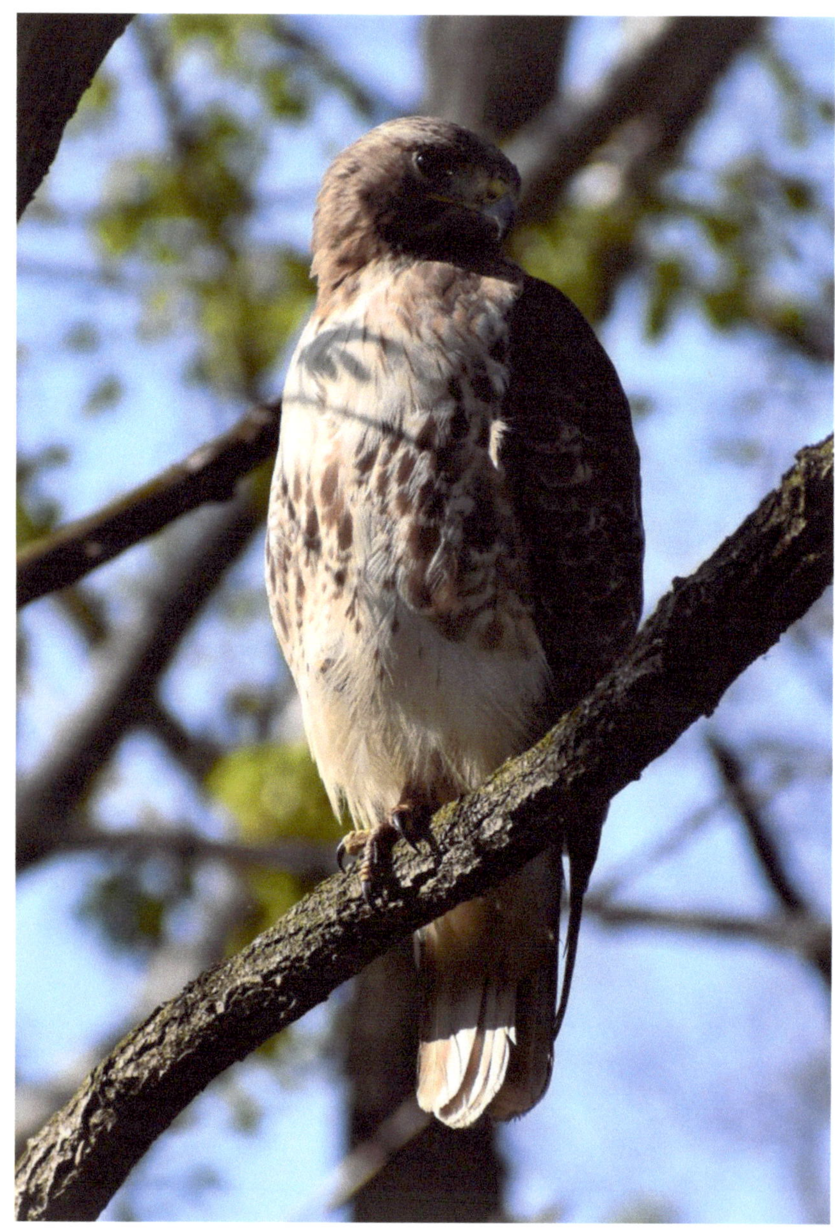

There is surviving an illness, and
there is thriving beyond the illness.
This person is known as a surthriver!

You can be many things to different
people, but you should be only one
thing to yourself: true.

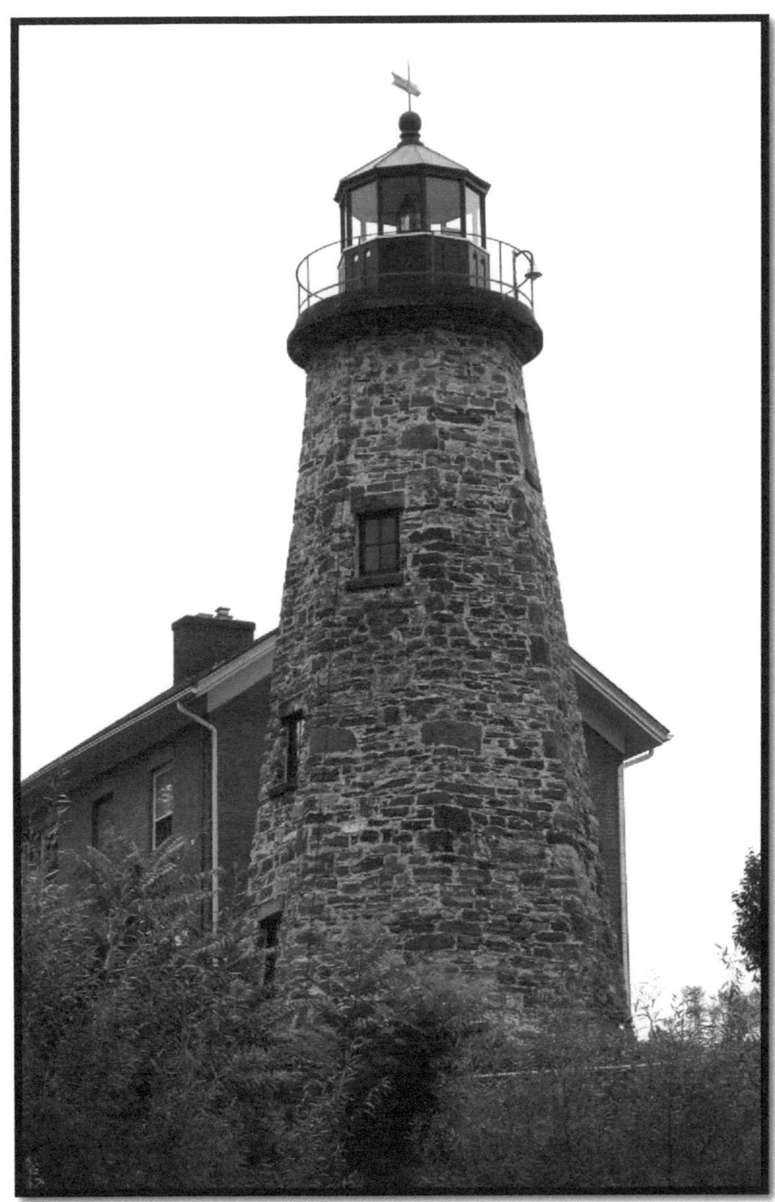

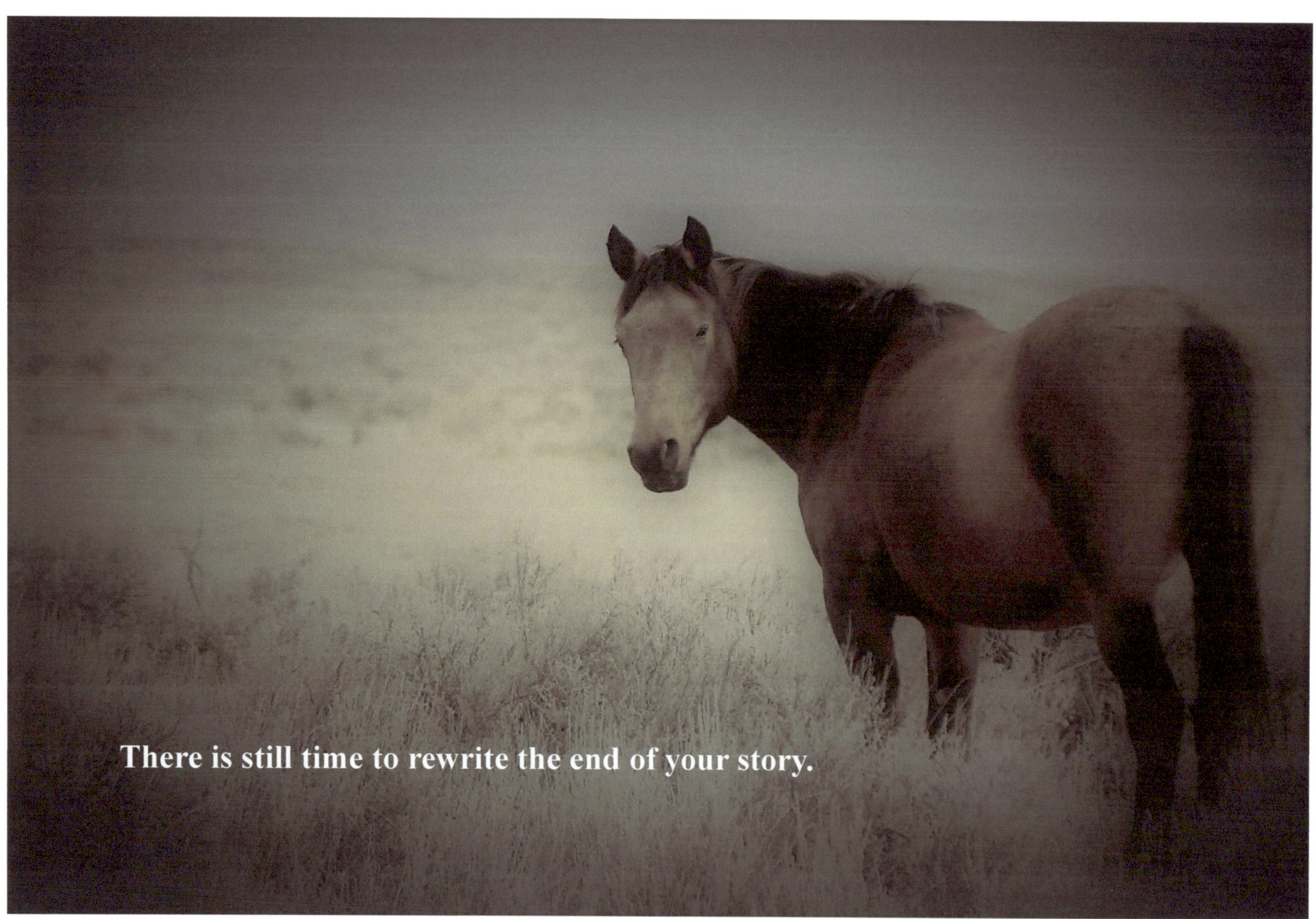
There is still time to rewrite the end of your story.

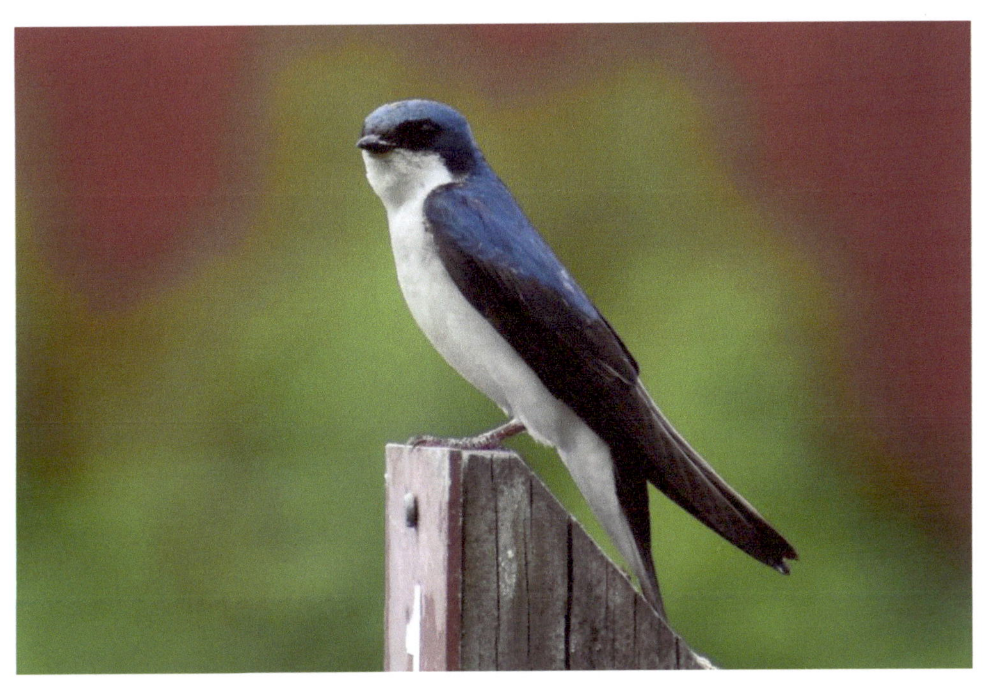

Experience is better than an Ivy
League education.

Children learn by watching;
what are you teaching them?

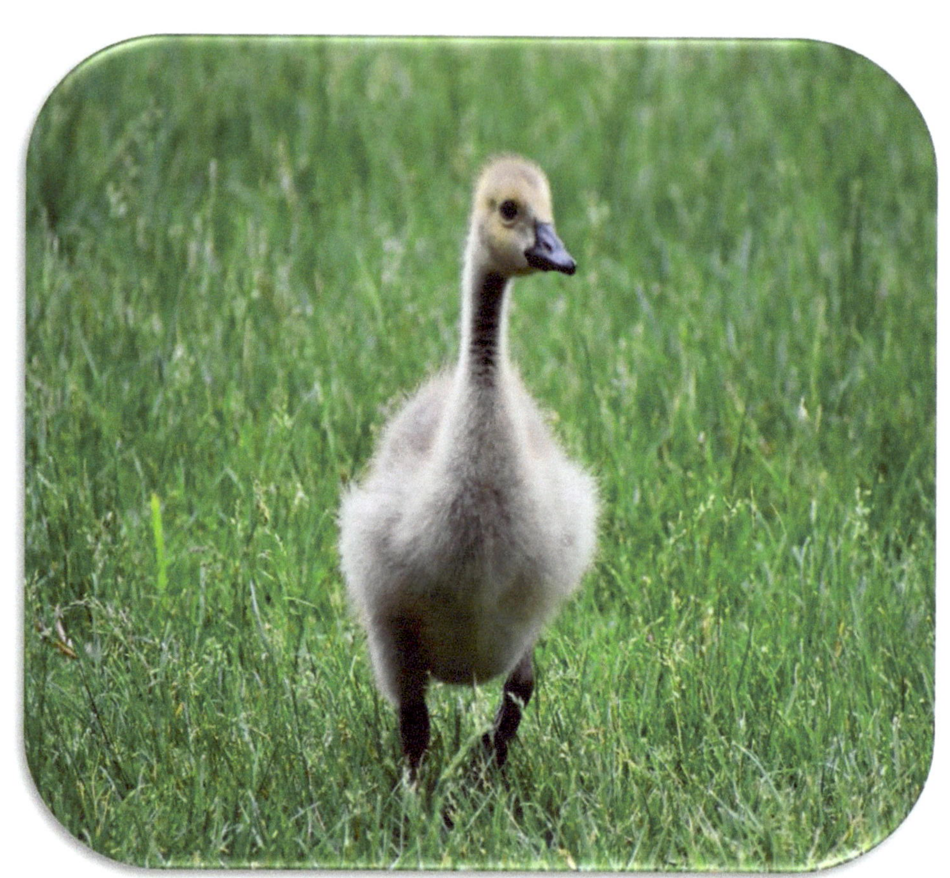

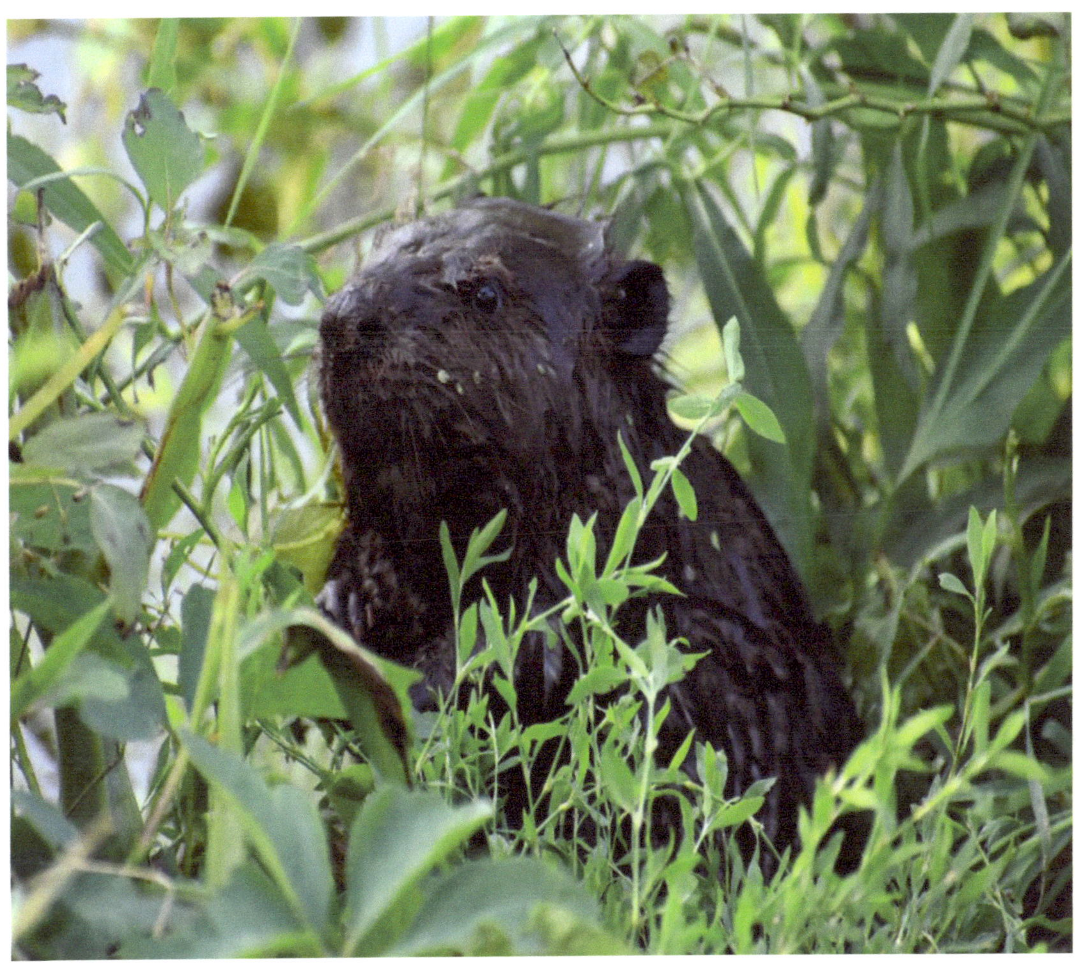

Never let kindness get confused with weakness.

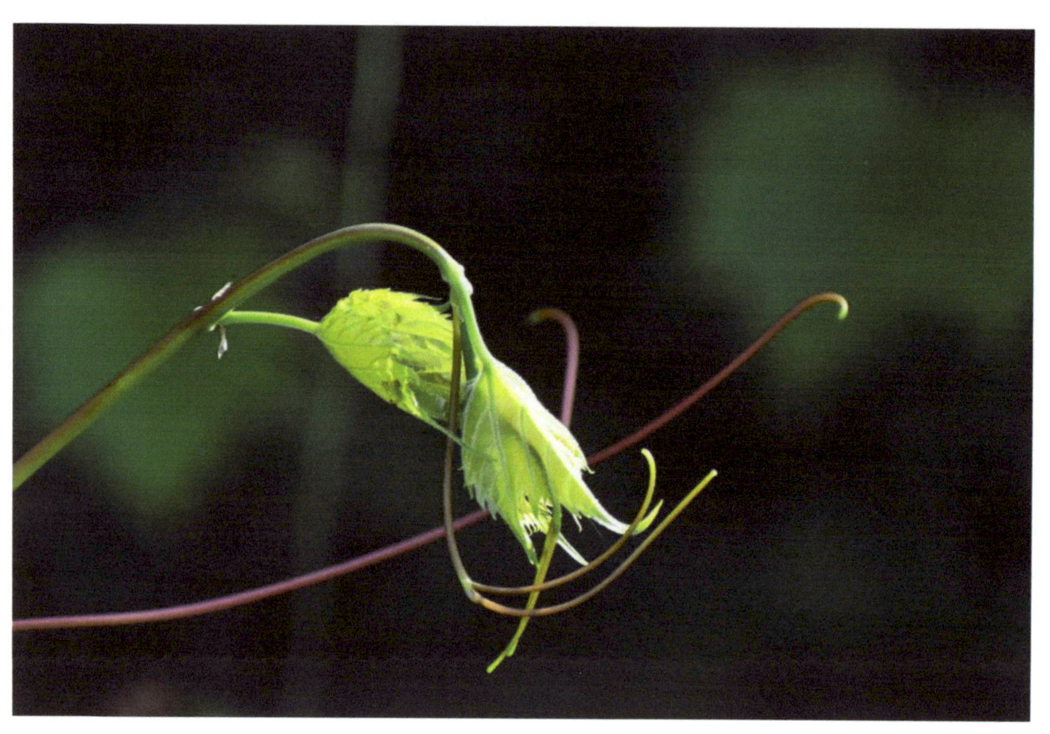

Never settle:

For second best

For being just enough

For hoping without trying

Unfulfilled dreams

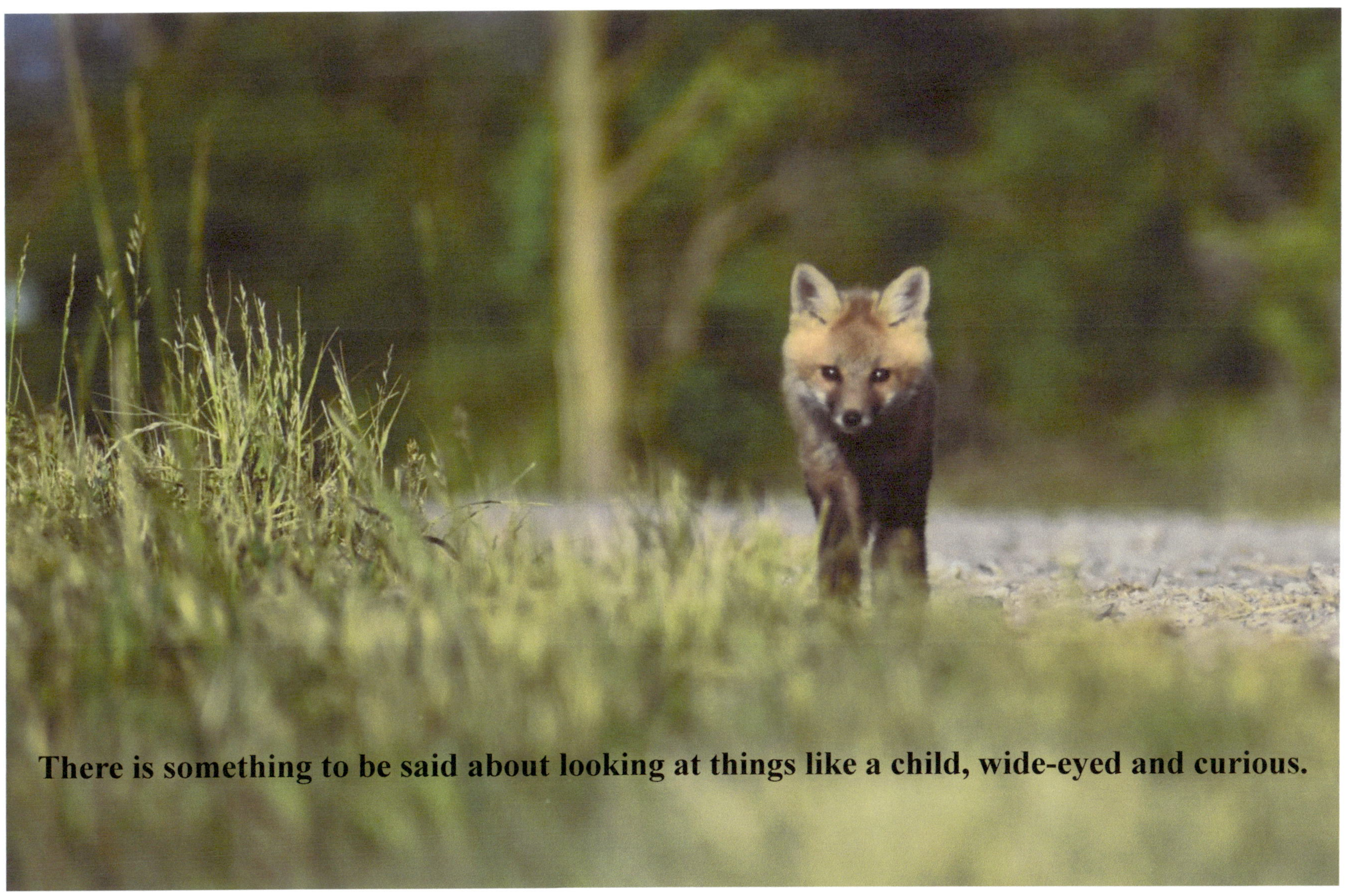

There is something to be said about looking at things like a child, wide-eyed and curious.

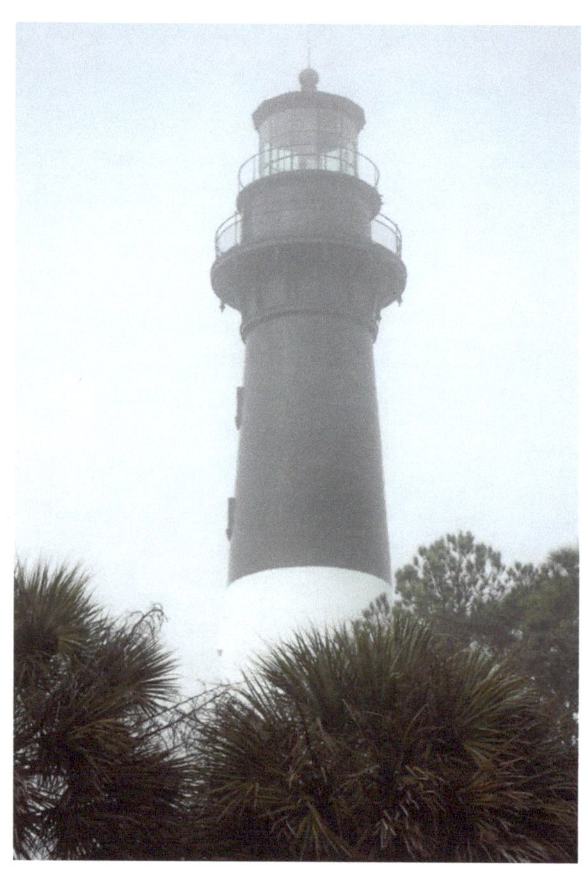

If you think about your life, it's kind of like the weather. There are good days, sunny and bright, where you are glad to be alive. There are stormy days that come and may stay a while, but eventually things get better. And then there are our major disasters, things that we wish we'd never have to go through. But life isn't like that. It is not all fresh air and sunshine.

Fair-weather friends are the people who love to be around fun people. They are there on your sunny days where everything is easy and bright. They show up to your birthday parties, your picnics, and holidays. They hug, and air kiss, and tell you just how much you mean to them. Until your weather gets a little dark. It is then that they tuck themselves into their homes all nice and snug so they don't get rained on.

Your thunderstorm friends are the people who show honest concern. They listen, they advise, and they will lend a hand if they can. They send cards when you're sick or flowers while you're in the hospital. They will offer to do whatever you need … they just don't show up on their own and do it, you have to ask.

If you are lucky, you have at least one hurricane friend. This is the person who will be right there when the storm clouds start to gather. When the wind lashes against your will and the waves are about to take you under. These are the people who will stand with you after your storm and help you pick up the pieces of your broken soul.

"I can," "I'll try," are weak
when compared to "I will."

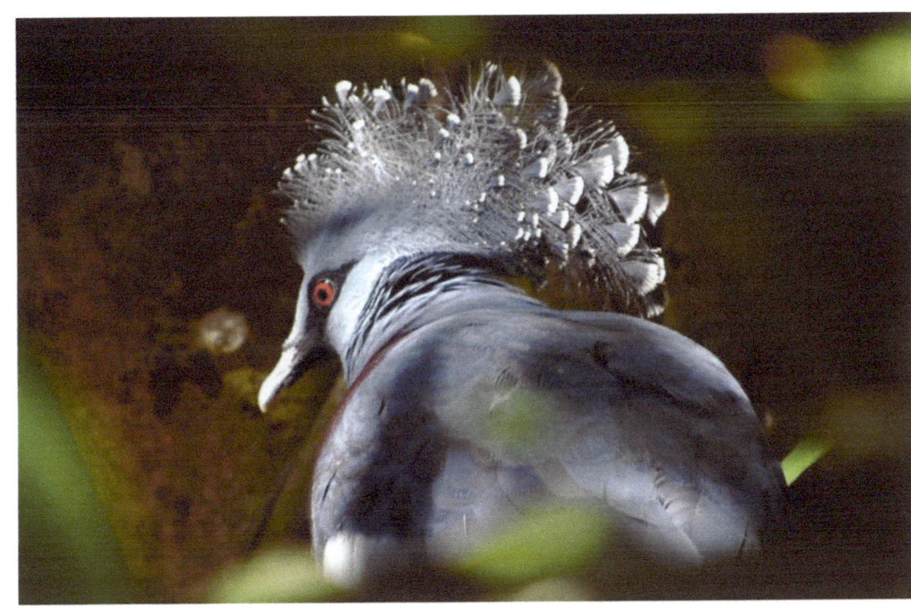

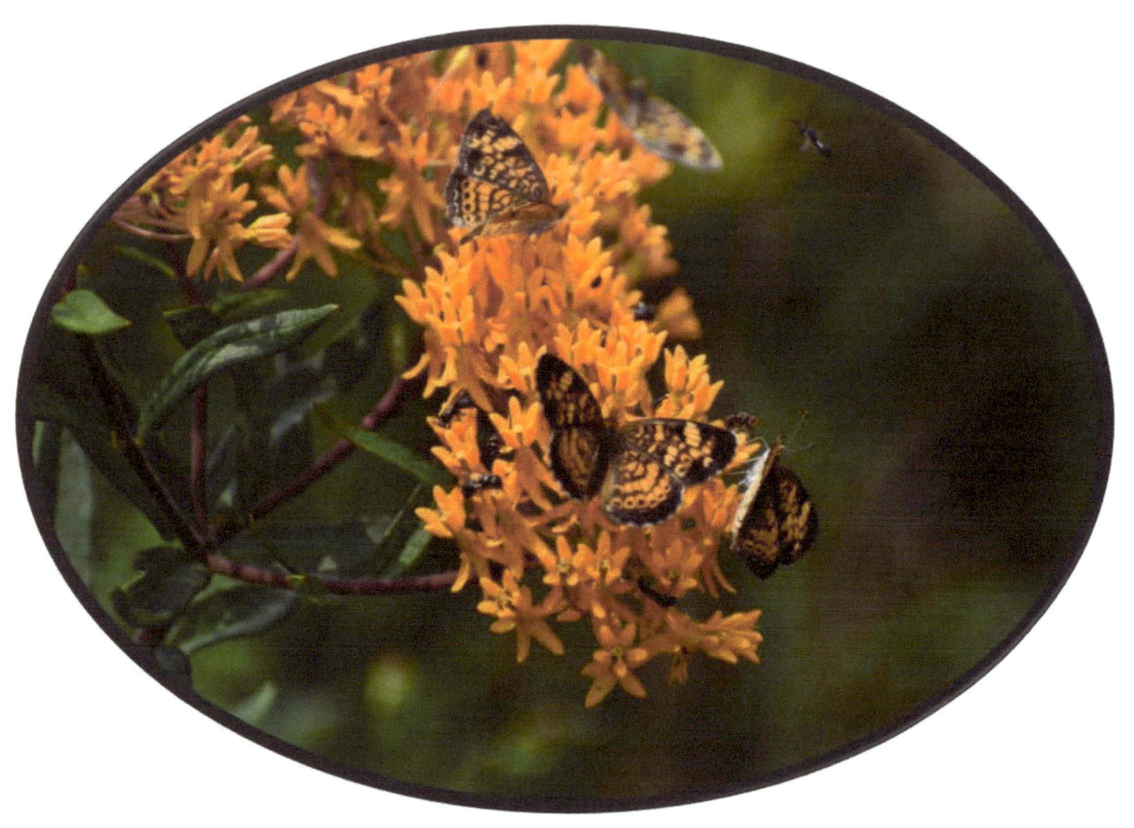

Peace comes from understanding
that you cannot "fix" everyone.

Encourage a child's
"might be."

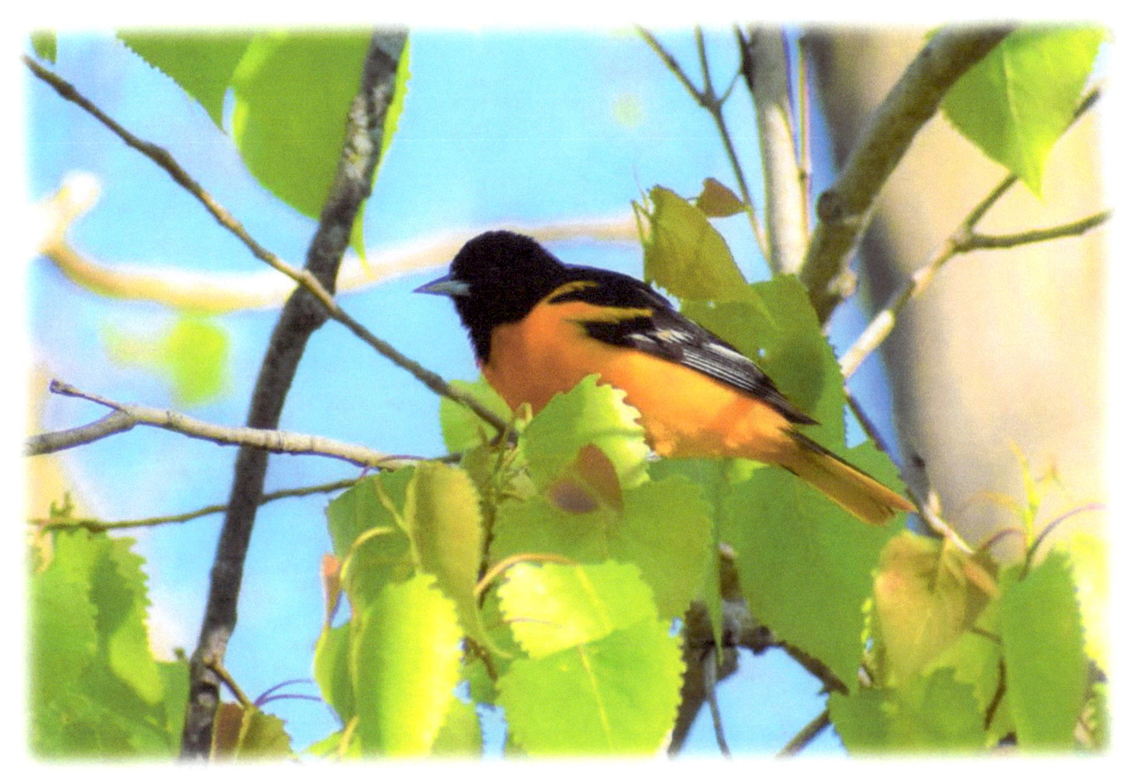

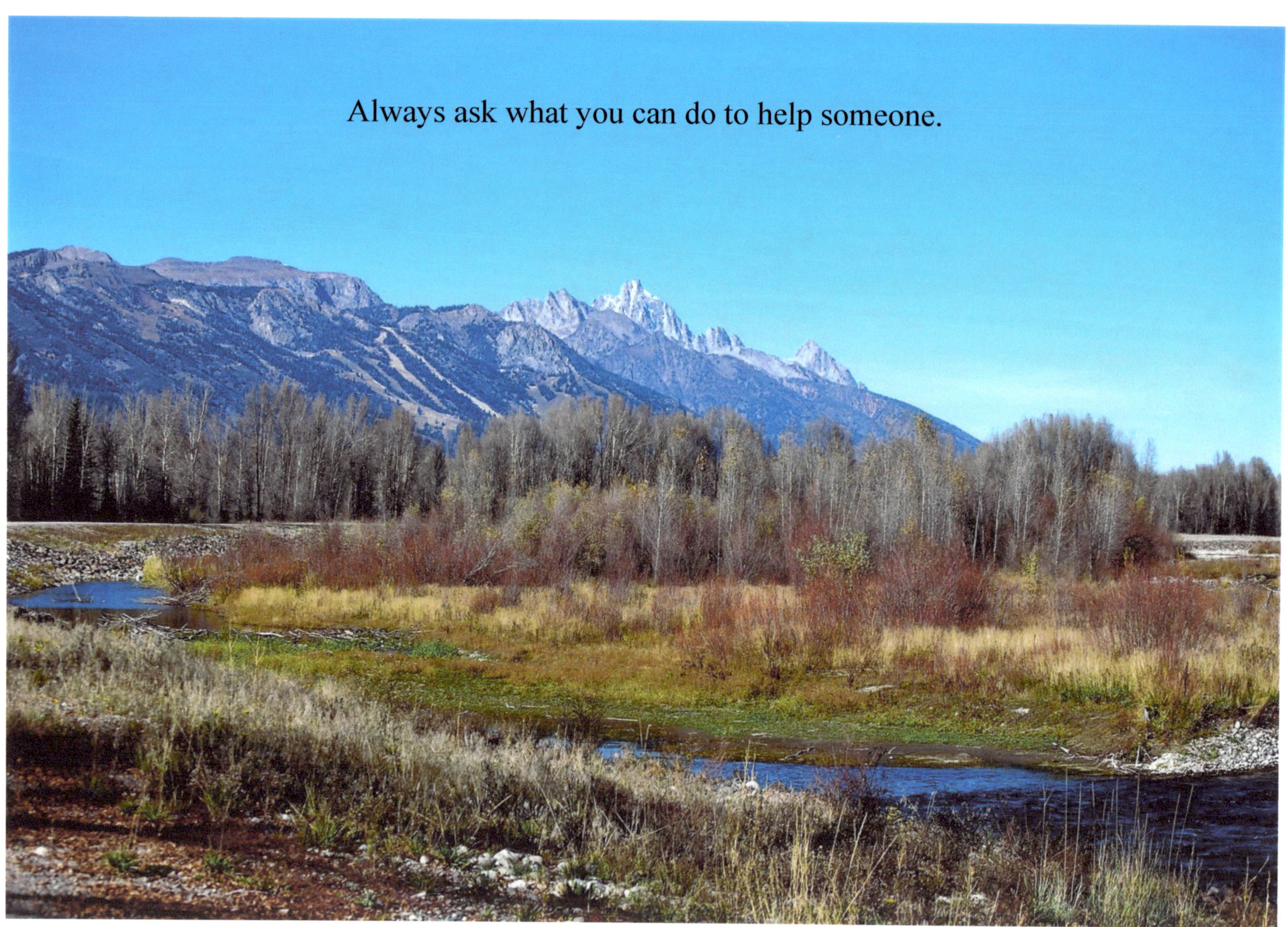

Always ask what you can do to help someone.

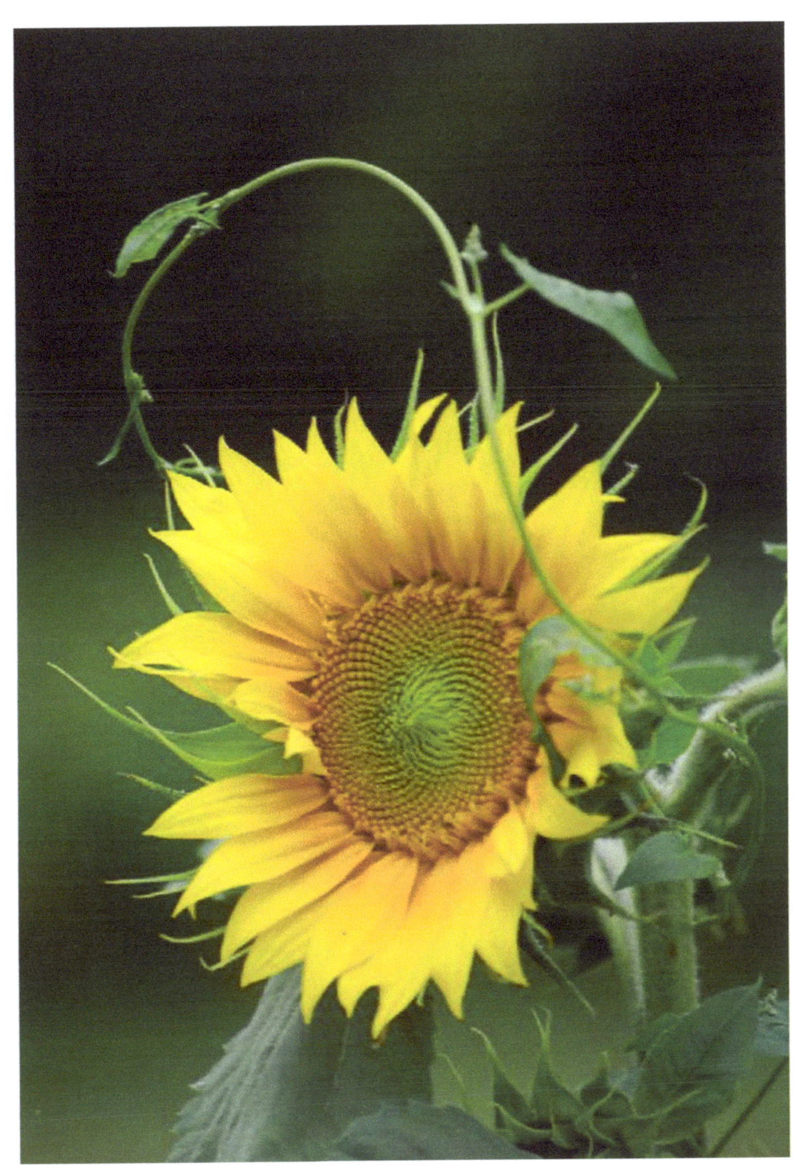

Do the hard. Someday, the world will throw it at you when you least expect it. Be prepared.

If you only use one affirmation,
use this: "I matter."

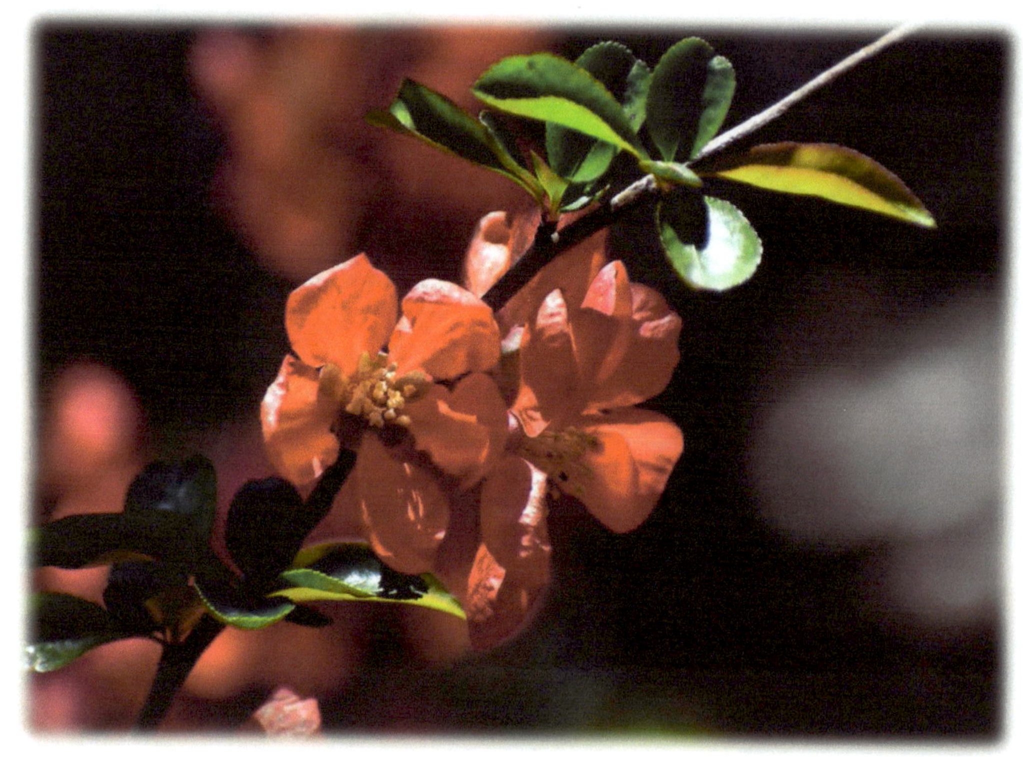

Being brave doesn't mean you aren't afraid. It means you do the brave thing in spite of the fear.

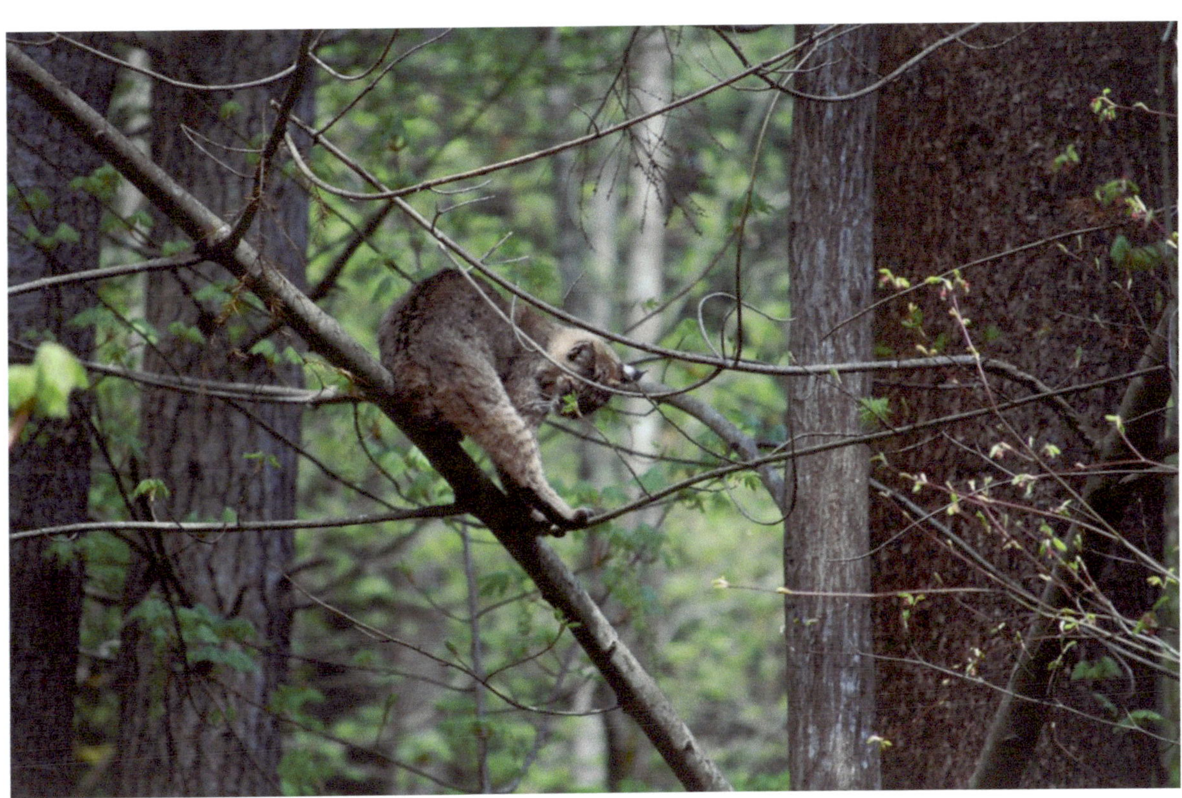

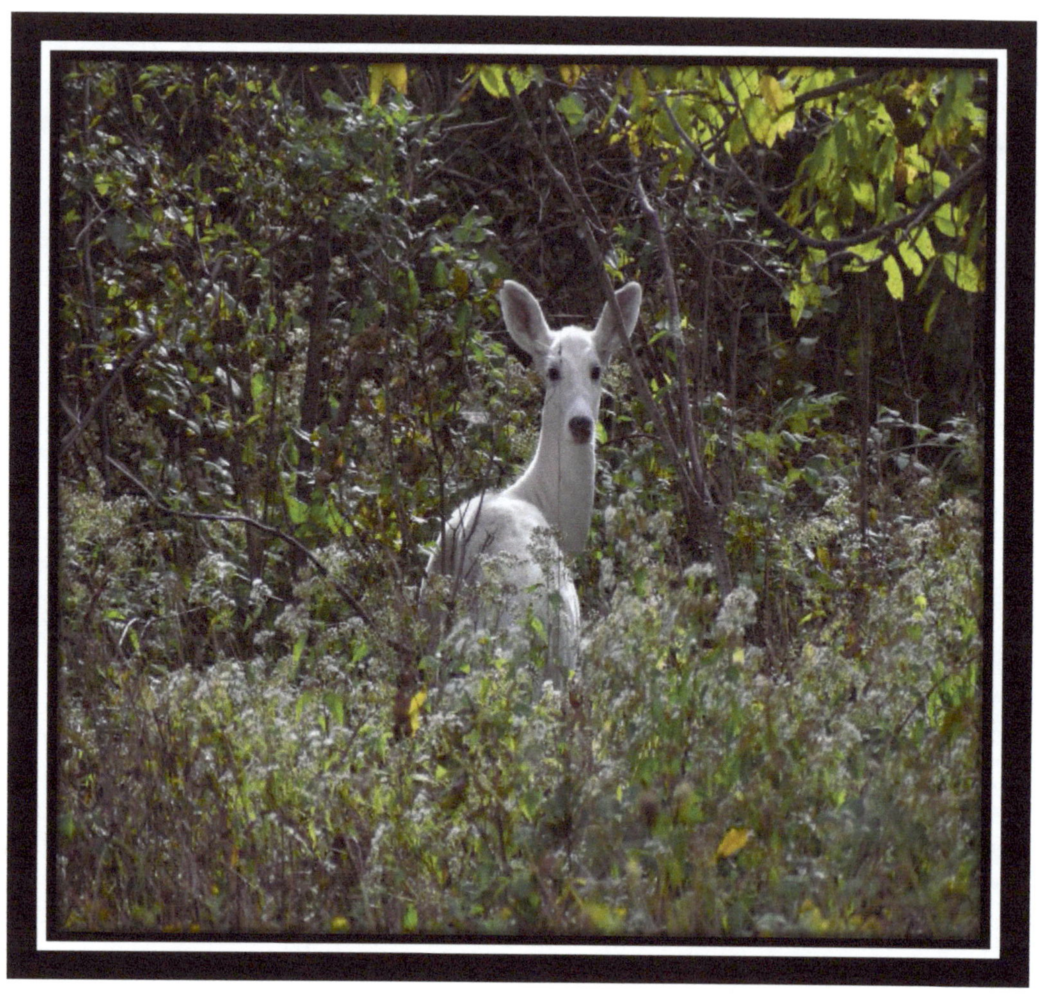

If you want to knock the wind out of someone's sails, apologize sincerely for what you have done.

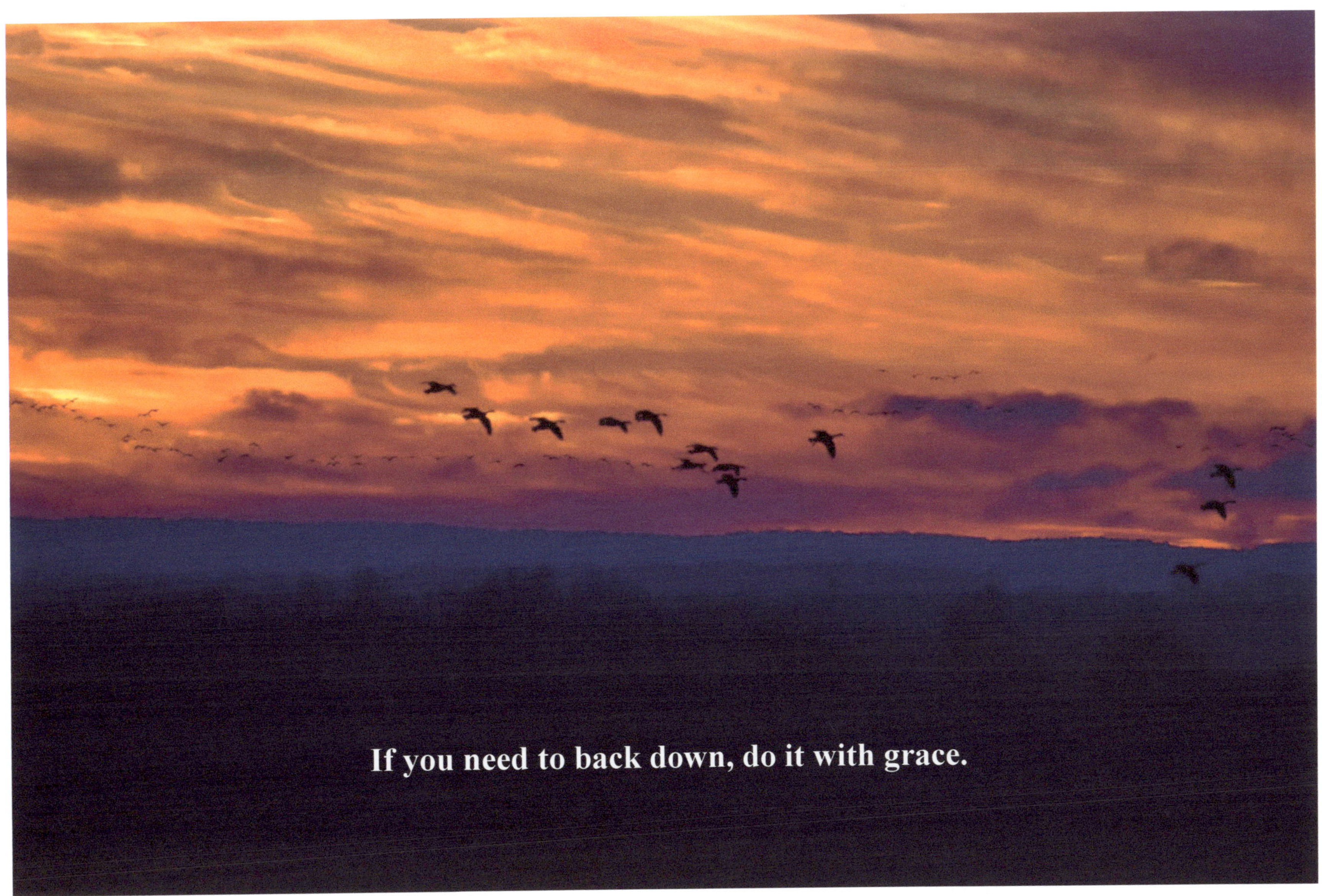

If you need to back down, do it with grace.

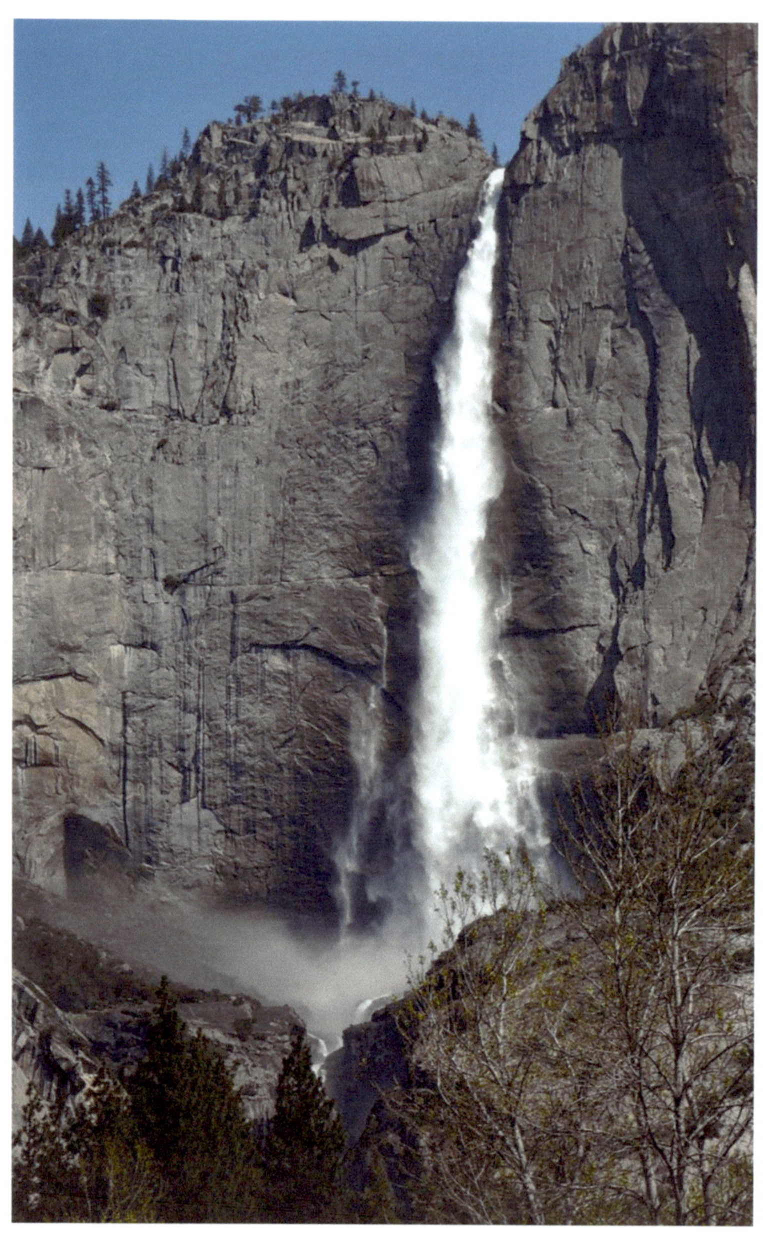

If you are going to learn any sign
language, make it "thank you."

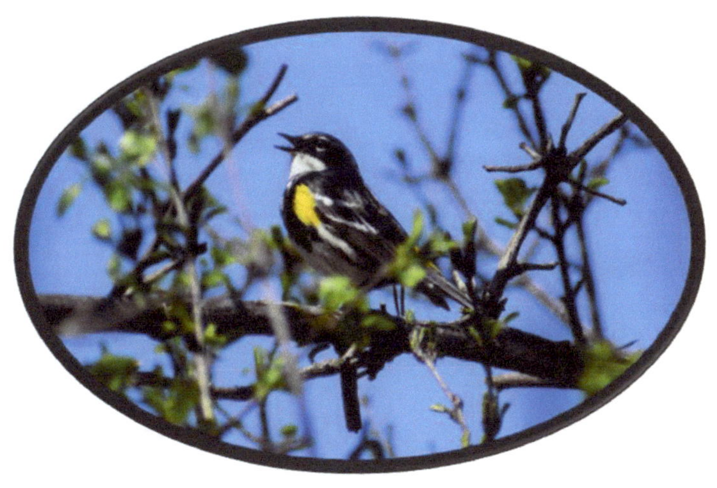

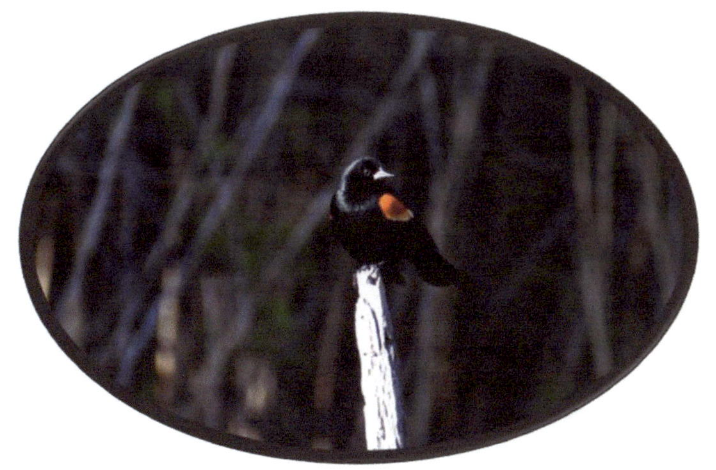

Often the "last straw" can be as light as a feather.

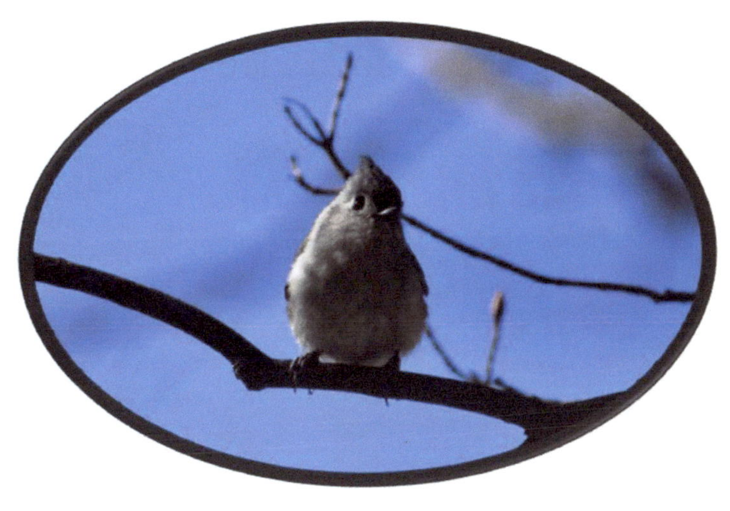

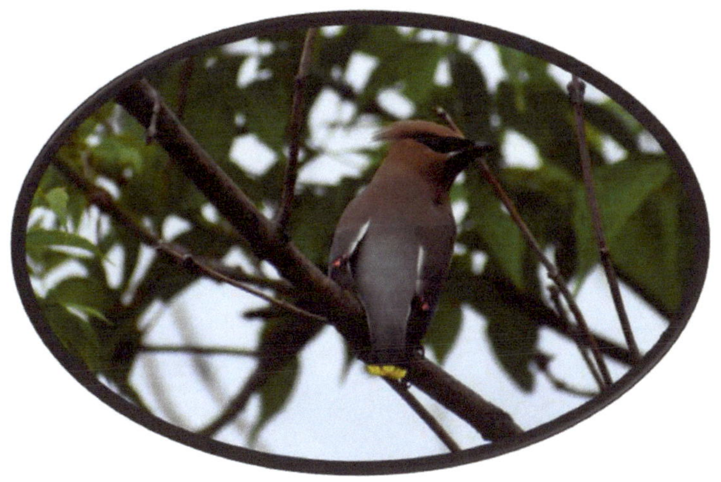

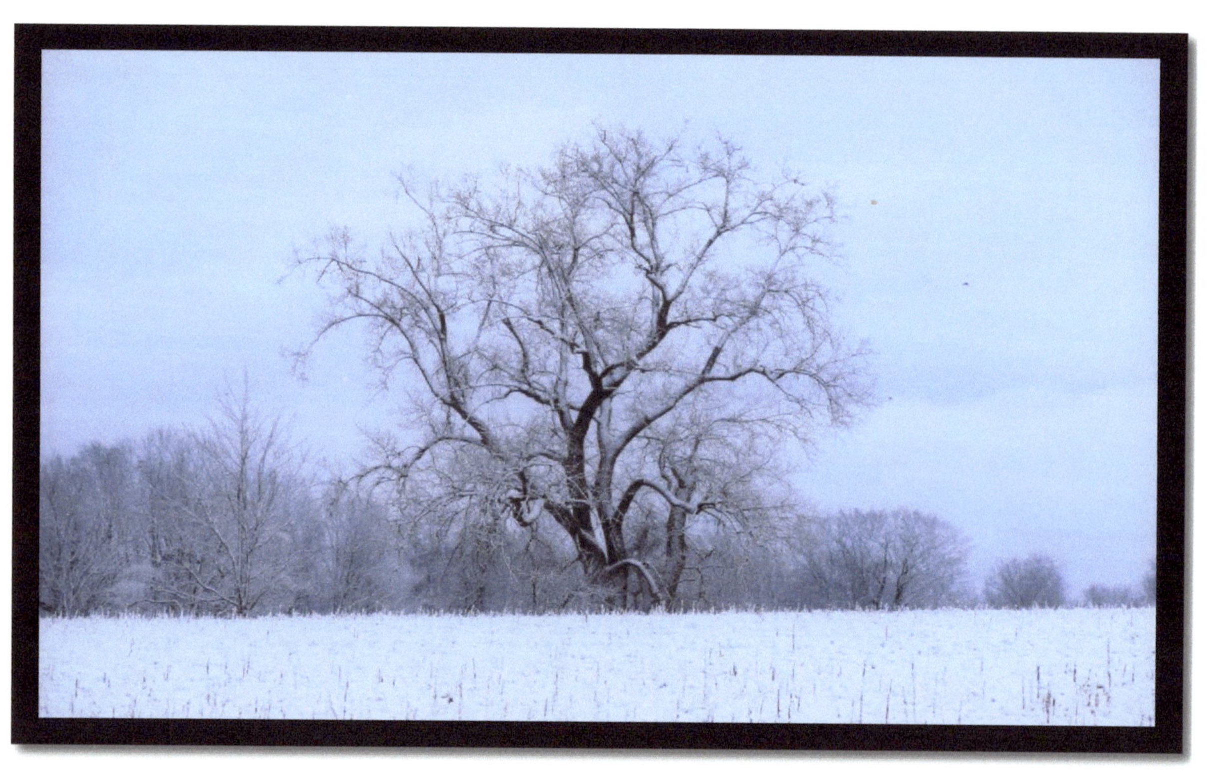

May your life be filled with:

Moments of comfort

Great memories

Lots of love

Good food

And fuzzy socks

Don't ask: "How much more, God?"
... because He always answers you.

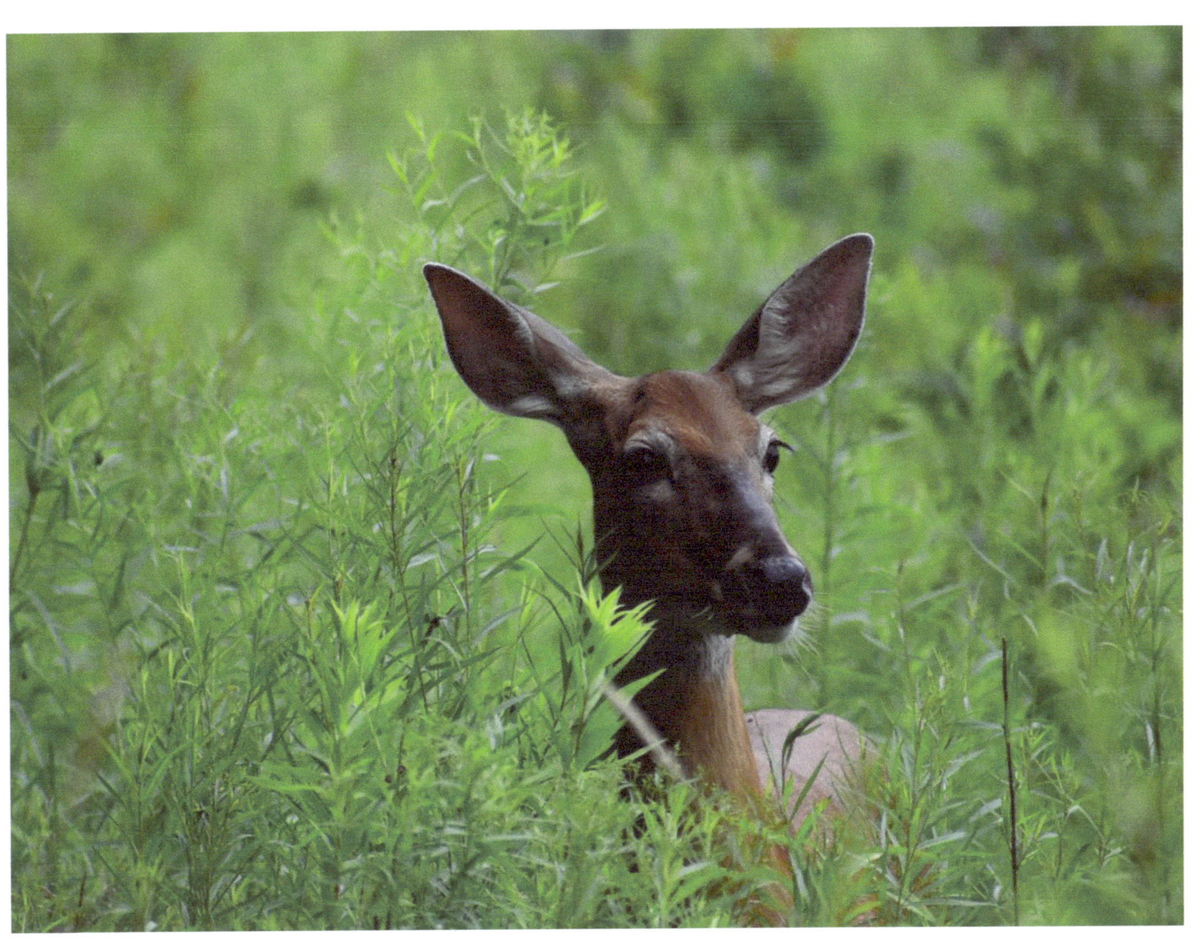

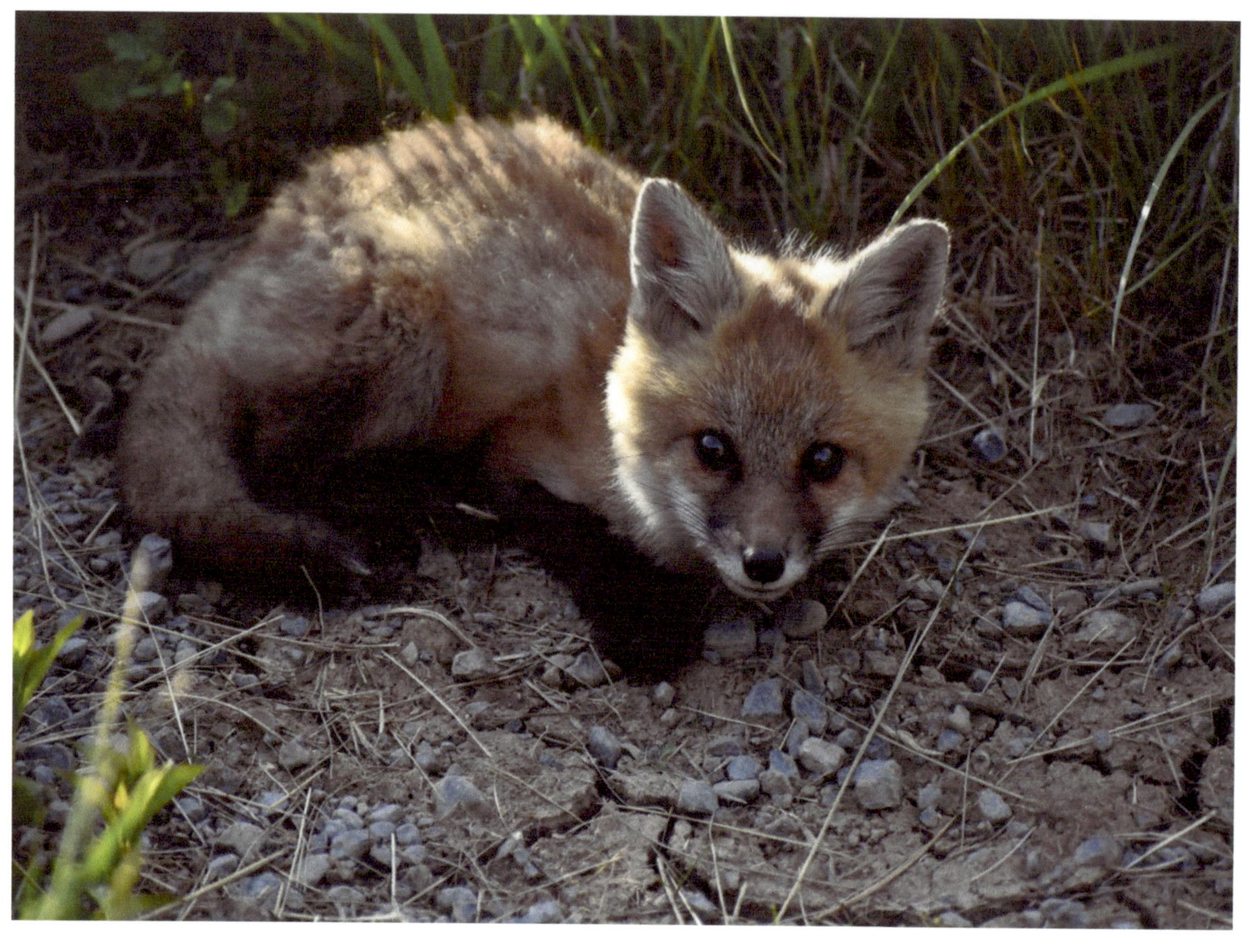

Never lose your sense of wonder.

In the year of the twentieth anniversary of my cancer diagnosis, I have been thinking about several things. Obviously, being blessed beyond measure is the first thing that comes to mind. The fact that I am still here, that God intervened and said "not now," isn't lost on me for even a moment.

This fact always makes me pause; it makes me wonder why. I have heard it said: "The two best days in your life are the day you were born, and the day you figure out why." I'm still looking for my why.

Another thing I think about is how people react to their diagnosis. There have been songs and movies, books and poems written about it. You know… "live like you were dying." These people take the news that there is a possibility they will die, and go out and do all the things they have wanted to do but haven't because life got in the way. They empty their bucket lists, make amends to others, put their affairs in order. They "show" their cancer that they are going to do whatever they can and live!

There are others who, once they hear their news, give up.
They resign themselves that nothing can be done.
They live in fear for the day that is inevitable and,
although they may put on a brave face, if you look
closely, you can see deep in their eyes that they, in fact,
have given up.

Some take the information and make the conscious decision to do whatever they can to fight the disease and give it up to God.

Ultimately, the way people deal with this information is really their reaction to the fact that their life might end. I'd remind myself of something else I have learned: No one is born with an expiration date stamped on their backside. So, it is critical to live your life—not in spite of death, not in fear of it, but because of it. Because it will happen; we just don't know when. So, live your life with purpose and with intention.

You don't have to live each day to the fullest; you'd be exhausted in a week. You don't have to be a superhero … we know none of us are. What we should do, however, is live each day kindly. Be respectful of others' opinions, perceptions, and choices. Try our best to see the good, not only in others but in ourselves. Listen with compassion.

I hope that you remember that each day is a gift. Don't hold off on doing what you want, what you love, or what you have always wished. Tomorrow is not promised to you.

I hope that you never have to face death before you are ready, but if you do, I hope that you have done all you wanted. That you are able to say: I have no regrets.

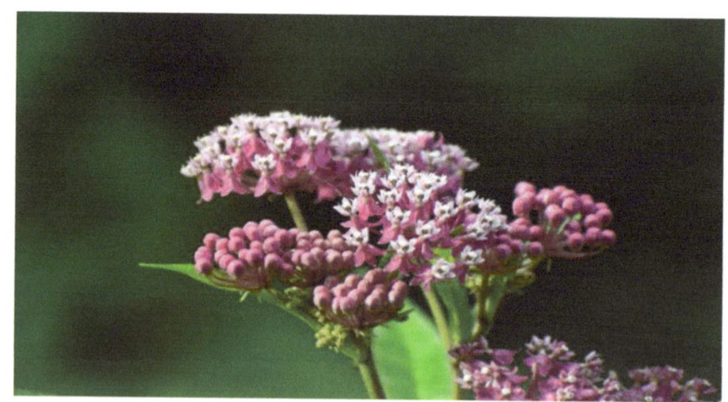

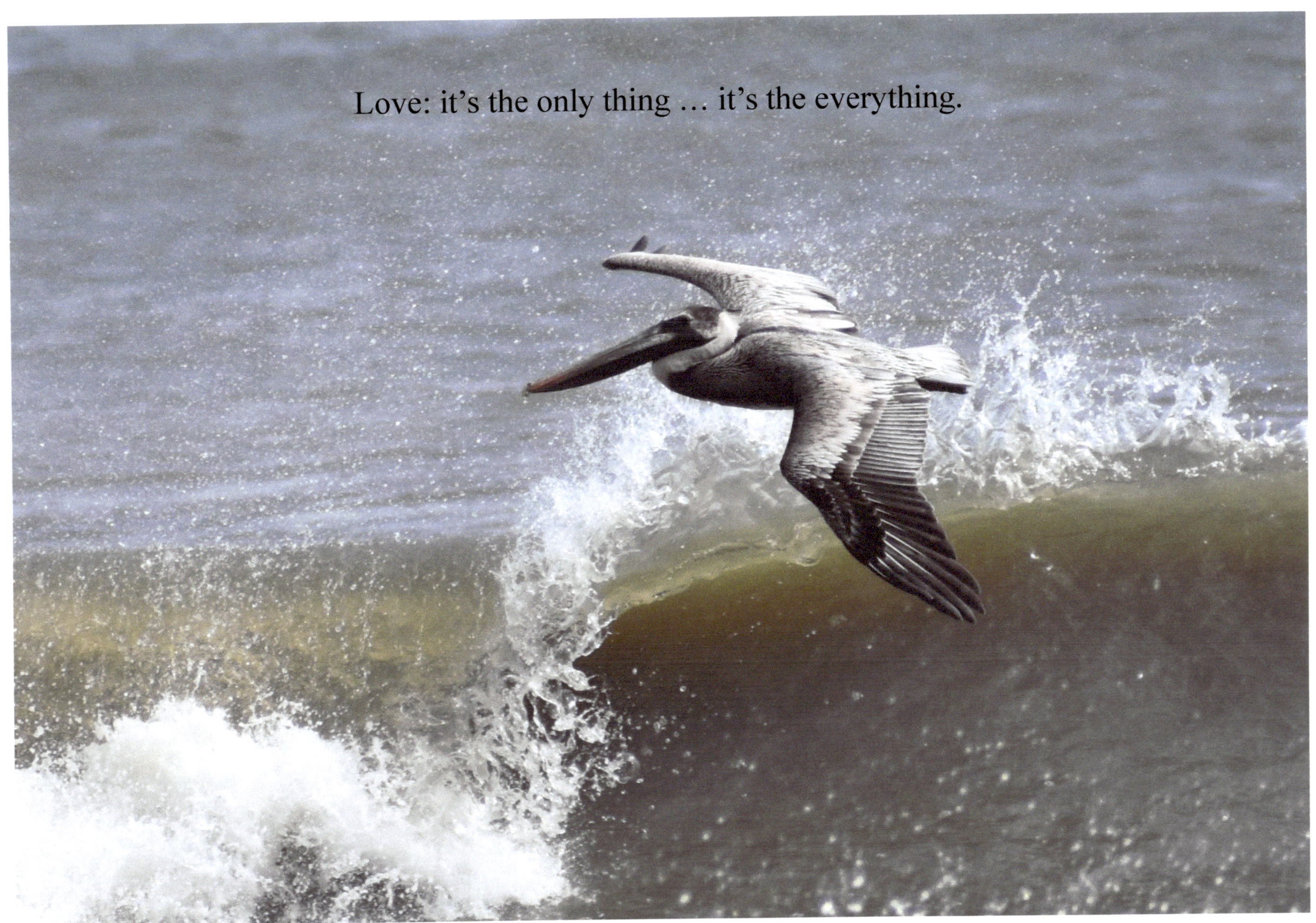

Love: it's the only thing … it's the everything.

So, in the end it really is all about perseverance. Being able to move forward with one foot in front of the other.

I am a cancer survivor, wife, daughter, sister, bonus grandmother, nature lover, and a traveling fool. My camera is either on my lap while I co-pilot or slung around me as I walk. I am always observing life as it unfolds around me.

My hope is that you enjoyed my photos and found just one saying that will inspire something in you. Or at least make you think or smile.

I am a firm believer that life is a matter of choices, some we like, some we don't. But if we make them, learn from them, and keep trying we will get what we want or what we need. Be gentle with yourself and others. We are all in this together.

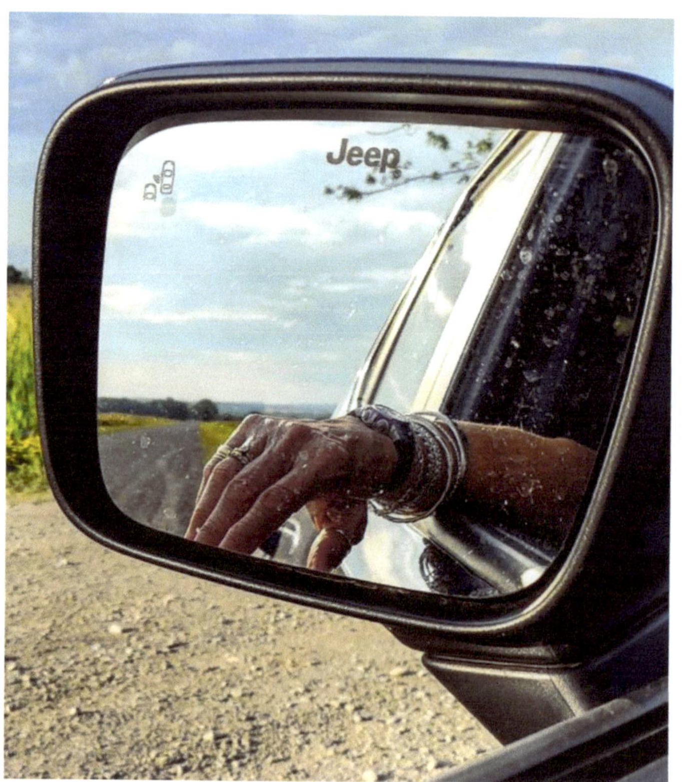